Work Values of Indian School Children

About the Author

Dr. Arun Kumar Tiwari (D. Phil. from Allahabad) is Associate Professor in Psychology at K.S. Saket P.G. College, Ayodhya affiliated to Dr. R.M.L. Awadh University, Faizabad. He has been continuously engaged in research works. He has directed a number of research projects sponsored by U.G.C., NCERT, and ICSSR as Principal Investigator/Director. Presently, he is collaborating in a Mega-Project of ICSSR with leading Professors of different Universities and IITs. He has written extensively on issues concerning organizational behaviour, health psychology, social psychology, and educational psychology. He has to his credit a good number of research papers published in various journals of repute. He has contributed independent chapters in six edited books. He himself has edited a book, entitled: *Psychological Perspectives on Social Issues and Human Development (2009)*; published by Concept. Also, he has written several articles on issues concerning the problems of day-to-day life, which are published in leading newspapers and popular magazines. He is the Chief Editor of a biannual journal, namely, *United Journal of Awadh Scholars (UJAS)*.

Work Values of Indian School Children

Arun Kumar Tiwari
Associate Professor,
Department of Psychology
K.S. Saket P.G. College, Ayodhya
Faizabad (U.P.)

CONCEPT PUBLISHING COMPANY PVT. LTD.,
NEW DELHI-110059

(A publication subsidy of Rs. 20,000 only was sanctioned by N.C.E.R.T., New Delhi, facilitated the publication of this book. The author acknowledges it with due gratitude).

ISBN-13: 978-81-8069-998-6

First Published 2014

Published and Printed by

Concept Since 1974

Concept Publishing Company Pvt. Ltd.
A/15-16, Commercial Block, Mohan Garden
New Delhi-110059 (India)
T: 25351460, 25351794, *F*: 091-11-25357109
E: publishing@conceptpub.com, W: www.conceptpub.com
Editorial Office: H-13, Bali Nagar, New Delhi-110 015, India.

Cataloging in Publication Data--*Courtesy:* D.K. Agencies (P) Ltd. <docinfo@dkagencies.com>

Tiwari, Arun Kumar.
Work values of Indian school children / Arun Kumar Tiwari.
p. cm.
Includes bibliographical references (p) and index.
ISBN 9788180699986

1. Work—Study and teaching (Middle school)—India. 2. Values—Study and teaching (Middle school)—India. 3. Junior high school students—India. I. Title.

DDC 331.072054 23

Foreword

Education, work and living have been theme of study of researches for a long time, across several disciplines. One of the dominant perspectives has emerged from Economist as they compute economic value of different streams and levels of education. Economic consequences of work and values are extremely important, but how they impact individuals, organisations and society goes far beyond the economic consequences. In such studies, work is linked to earning, supposed to be an important aspect of status and material prosperity. While this may be true, it is also true that economic satisfaction can be self-limiting and does not go beyond a point if it does not include aspects like values, relationship and larger goals of life. If work does not get associated with feeling of accomplishment, meaning in life and promotion of social well-being, economic benefits of works may be limited or can be counter productive for societies and nations. This is a complex question, and answer may seem like a serendipitous search for both, those who have the economic status and those who want to have it.

Societies and communities are changing faster than anticipated and so is the nature of employment, relationships and organizations. One often notices that 'online communities' formed through internet and social networking sites are as important or probably become more important than the real ones. Similarly, tension between job and family has always been there but currently when individuals migrate from place to place, from one country to another, this has acquired an entirely different dimension. Then the question arises—what is the community to which one belong and how does one connect to it? Hence, the meaning of what is desirable for individuals and communities becomes contentious to define and more difficult to acquire. There is little doubt that early years contribute immensely to the development of values. So what do children think about their life and work can be immensely important for future. Not enough research has been conducted in this field in India. In this context the present study is a very welcome addition.

The study, as evident from the extensive review of literature, is rooted in Indian values and culture but takes into account the current empirical and theoretical evidence. Family as the first and important source of development of work values has been given due importance in the study but school and education have been well placed in the formulation of main research questions. Also, analysis of textbooks as a source of inculcating of work values is notable. Curriculum for schools is designed by experts and delivered by teachers in school. In this whole chain, textbooks are critical link which impact the children. Along with this, views of parents, teachers and school administrators as important stakeholders have been given centre space in the study. Development of scale for measuring work values among junior high school children coming from rural and urban background is one of the important highlights of the study. All these aspects have provided a depth to the study which cover a wide range of issues.

The findings of studies are an important reminder to school leaders, educationist, policy-makers and parents about the need to reflect and reorient themselves towards the kind of work values we want our children to have. This will determine the kind of society we will have in future. The study, it is hoped, will not only inform all stakeholders about the current state but will also give impetus to more research in this area and pave the way to fresh thinking about the issues related to development of values in our country, particularly among children.

Rajeev Sharma,
Ravi J. Matthai Centre for Educational Innovation
Indian Institute of Management, Ahmedabad

Acknowledgements

The reported project was financially supported by the NCERT, New Delhi as an ERIC project. I would like to express my deep gratitude to this institution of excellence. At the level of initial planning of the project, the ERIC associated with the Department of Educational Research and Policy Perspectives (DERPP) of this institution provided me many valuable suggestions. For that I am highly grateful to all the expert members of ERIC and also to the members of DERPP. I am also grateful to the expert Evaluator—appointed by NCERT, who not only approved my work for publication, but also provided me several suggestions to improve the draft of this report. I must acknowledge that I have been benefited by his expert suggestions in modifying the report.

I take this opportunity to express my deep regards to Prof. G. Mishra, who has been a great source of motivation for many of his students—including myself. Prof. Mishra helped me in various ways at different stages of the project. Further, I thank Prof. Rajeev Sharma of IIM, Ahmedabad for his useful suggestions. Also he was generous to write a Foreword for this book.

My research supervisor Prof. R.C. Tripathi has not only guided my D. Phil. Research work, he has given me his expert guidance in every stage of my career. I am really indebted to him. This is the only indebtedness, which I regard a proud privilege of mine. The title of the present book is suggested by Prof. Tripathi.

My departmental colleagues of my employing college also deserve appreciation for their help at different occasions. Shri Shailendra Kumar Yadav served the project as a Junior Project

Fellow. I want to bring it on record that he worked in the project with full dedication and made my task easy. I wish him every success in his life. I dedicate this book to my parents Shri Shankar Saran and Smt. Gulab, who virtually forced me to stay with academic career which I am enjoying most now.

Many institutions and individuals alongwith the students and their guardians helped us in collection of relevant information for the project. They all deserve our special thanks and regards. Finally, I express my sincere thankfulness to the Concept Publishing Company Pvt. Ltd., New Delhi-110059 and its proprietor Shri Ashok Kumar Mittal for acceptance of our draft to publish. The Concept has produced many volumes of repute in various scientific disciplines. I believe that the new book would be appreciated by the researchers and also by the parents, teachers and other stakeholder associated with early educational system. With regards and all the best wishes to all.

Ram Navami, **Arun Kumar Tiwari**
1st April, 2012.

Introduction

Human Capital theory—proposed in the fields of industrial/organizational sciences, views human capabilities, their knowledge, skills, talents, efforts, and work habits as integral part of the capital of an organization along with its financial and physical resources. India—as a nation—is also an organization. It has projected a vision of an agenda of development for 2020. This agenda can be realized only when the nation develops a human capital of great quality. Here, the educationists and social scientists have major role to play. They will have to explore the means and modalities to develop such human capital. For this purpose, educational institutions appear as one of the most important sites for relevant interventions.

The work habits and work values would be an integral part of such human capital. It is unfortunate that despite strong advocacies in favour of dedication and hard work by leading leaders of different fields—including religio-philosophical, political, economic, etc.—we Indians do not value 'work' very much. *Aram* culture is still dominating Indian people. We shirk working hard and value *Aram* rather than the work. It seems that the nation in general has not been able to establish and promote work values among its citizens. Now if we have to reach the target set by 'Agenda 2020', we have to analyze and investigate the scenario in order to prepare appropriate strategies of interventions to transform the situation. One purpose of such interventions should be to develop appropriate and progressive work values among the citizens of our country. The studies have revealed that the work values form particularly during childhood and adolescence. The work values formed during these stages of development are found to be relatively stable over time. On the basis of such findings in their studies, the researchers and other academicians have advocated to work for such a curriculum at elementary education system that may inculcate the essential values among the students of these levels. The same is true for the inculcation of work values also. The work values determine—how one feels (pleasure, anxiety, punished or stress) while working. A person develops work values by learning. This learning occurs either through socialization process (including the process of imitation, modelling and conformity) or educational processes. Thus, it is apparent that the education system can be used in order to generate positive work values.

With these presumptions, the present research project was planned in order to attend the following major objectives:

1. Identification of the work values available in curriculum—presently being taught at Jr. High School level.
2. Study the pattern of preferences and practices of work values prevailing among these students.
3. Examining the views of the stakeholders (e.g., parents, teachers, school administrators).
4. To develop a Work Values Scale for Jr. High School students.
5. Examining the variation in work values in relation to contextual variables (gender, rural-urban habitation and classes or grades).

The research was conducted in three Phases. In Phase 1, the textbooks of Hindi, English and Social Studies of grades 6th to 8th were content analyzed to find out the themes related to 'work'. Despite all the efforts and leniencies, only 83 references in total, were found where the work related themes were available in these textbooks. The number of these themes was 39 only. It was really a small number. It suggested including more numbers of themes containing references of work values in the syllabi.

In Phase 2, 30 students, 20 teachers, 30 parents and 20 administrative staff (serving in educational set-up) were interviewed with the help of a semi-structured interview schedule, which consisted questions about the meaning of work, attitude towards work and work values. The obtained information were analyzed and some very interesting results were found. For example, 73 per cent of respondents were of the view that the students of classes 6th to 8th understand the meaning of work. These respondents also felt that if a student does not understand the meaning of work, he cannot be made responsible for the same. It is the lackness from the sides of guardians, teachers and society, which is to be blamed for this situation.

The Phase 3 was major part of the study. In this Phase, the first task was to develop a reliable and valid scale to measure work values of students at elementary level. This scale was developed and used at the next stage of this phase. The prime objective of this stage was to examine the variations in work values across some contextual variables. These variables were; gender, rural-urban habitation and grades of the students (class 6th, 7th and 8th). The results indicated that gender played more significant role. The female students were found to have higher work values in comparison to their male classmates. Interestingly, they did not differ with each other on domestic work value and home assignment value. The rural and urban students also did not differ on these two factors, but they showed patterns of differences on the rest of scores. Rural people had more positive feelings with works, whereas the scores on the knowledge through works were higher in urban students. The grades of the students also were found determining the variations in work values. The scores on the work values obtained in case of class 7th students were higher than that of class 6th, suggesting an improvement in work values at this stage. However, the scores of class 8th students were not different with the scores of class 7th students. It indicated stagnation in development of work values after class7th. From the effects of interactions among these three variables, only one interaction effect (between gender and class) was significant. The female students of class 6th and 7th scored higher in comparison to their male counterparts. Such difference was not obtained among class 8th students. It also suggested the above said stagnation after class 7.

The findings of the study were found to have several policy implications. For example, the groups of students, teachers, parents and administrative staff, when interviewed in this study, expressed the view that the children in general understand the meaning of work, but the children recognize the instrumental aspect of work only, in which it is believed that the work, when completed, gives some rewards of physical nature, such as money, meal or toy. They have no idea about the intrinsic aspect of work. Therefore, it can be suggested to make children aware about the intrinsic aspects of the work. The possibility of teaching them the 'skill' to work with a sense of non-attachment (*anasakti*) should also be explored.

The parents, teachers and administrative staff were found to concede that the students cannot be blamed for not having proper work values. It is failure of our system that has not been able to promote and nurture the work values among them. As the corrective measures, the entire education system should be revaluated focusing on its components that might have links with the development of work values. Also, the teachers should be given special training of instilling work values among their students. The parents should be provided suggestions and guidelines—useful in nurturing the work values of their children at guardians meet.

The results indicated that the development of work values gets stagnated after class 7th. The policy-makers should take notice of it. If it is true, the causes should be traced and action should be taken to remove them. The policy implications of other findings also are discussed in final report. This discussion can be of use for our policy-makers, parents and teachers in developing the strategies for instilling the adequate work values among our children who would shape the fate of our country in future.

Contents

List of Tables

List of Boxes

List of Figures

1

Work and Work Value in Specific Context of Children

Overview of Literature

Some years ago one advertisement of Tata Steel Company appeared in most of the leading national newspapers. In that advertisement a photo of some nicely uniformed people having confident look on their faces and standing in a orderly way, was shown followed by Company's slogan—'We make people. By the way we make steel too'. Of course, the Tata Steel Company is well-known name in the field of steel production, but the company, through this advertisement, wanted to be recognized for its works on its human component. Certainly it was unequivocal recognition of importance of Human Capital in an organization, which if combines with adequate raw materials, produces a quantity of quality products automatically; and makes the organization effective. Human capital is embodied in people working in the organization and is an amalgam of factors such as education, training, experience, intelligence, energy, work habits, trustworthiness and initiativeness. It is unconditionally accepted that an organization would have competitive edge over others only if the human resources are optimally utilized by it. A nation also is a type of organization. Therefore, a nation also needs 'people of good qualities' for its full effectiveness. The same is true for India. India, as a development-lusting nation, has projected a vision of an agenda of development for 2020. This agenda can be realized only when the nation develops a human capital of great quality. For this purpose, the nation would need active cooperation from different academic disciplines, along with the governmental initiatives. Each of these disciplines, including education and other social sciences should accept this challenging task and should move forward with its share of contributions, enabling the nation to achieve its declared agenda of development.

While focusing on development of a great human capital one needs to be aware that among the various attributes of Human capital, the values of people have special significance because in any organization, the organizational culture that has been found to be clearly associated with organizational success, gets manifested by the values of its people (Schein, 1985). This contention gets supported when we see that the Japanese people's possession of a more appropriate set of values than those held by individuals in other countries, has transformed a badly ruined country (during Second World War) into a strong and developed nation in a short period. At different occasions, the concerns have been expressed that the Indian people do not have such set of values. Since in absence of these values, the country would not be able to realize its objectives of development, it seems essential to make endeavours for inculcating appropriate values among Indians. For this, adequate strategies of interventions would be needed. It is unequivocally conceded that the educational institutions are one of the most important sites for relevant interventions in this connection. The study, reported in this report, was planned in the context of these arguments.

There should be no doubt that the work habits and work values would be an integral part of a human capital that would be required for desired national development. It is unfortunate that despite strong advocacies in favour of dedication and hard work by leading leaders of different fields, including religious-philosophical, political, economic, etc., we, the Indians, do not value 'work' very much due to the presence of so-called *Aram* culture in our society, where people shirk working hard unless induced to. Indians have been believed to value *Aram* (i.e., rest and relaxation) rather than hard work (Jai B.P. Sinha, 2008). The above scenario is in contrast to the place of work that has been traditionally given to work in the life space in Indian view. 'Work' has been called 'worship' and in textual and folk discussions, it has been assigned a creative role. Indian tradition has maintained the significance of work values since Vedic period (*kurvanneveh karmani jijeevichhatam samah*) and 'work' has been considered to be a criterion of *Yoga*. Not only this, excellence in work was given the complete status of *Yoga* (*Yogah karmasu kaushalam*). It has been operationalized at different times as *Karma*, *Kartavya*, *Udyog*, or *Sanskar* and have received detailed treatment in various streams of thoughts. Swami Ramsukh Das has opined that there is '*Swargadik* system' for pleasure or enjoyment (*Sukha*) and '*Narakadik System*' for pains or sufferings (*Dukha*). This *Lok* is not just for *Sukha* or *Dukha*, it is only for '*Karma*, i.e., work'. Mahatma Gandhi himself set an example of dedication and hard works. He had equal liking for all types of works. For him, no work was superior or inferior. Pandit Jawaharlal Nehru gave the slogan and demonstrated by his work habits that *Aram Haram Hai*. From economic field, one can see the example of Dhiru Bhai Ambani who, through his dedication and hard work, touched the heights of sky. It is really a matter of great concern that despite all such exemplary evidences, *Aram* culture is still dominating Indian people. They shirk working hard and value *Aram* rather than the work. It seems that the nation, in general, has not been able to establish and promote work values among its citizens. Now if we have to reach the target set by 'Agenda 2020', we have to analyze and investigate the scenario in order to prepare appropriate strategies of interventions to transform the situation. For this purpose, one needs answer of the question; why some people work harder than others? Partial explanation may be given through their work values. Furthermore, a person's values answer the question—"what is important to him"? In this sense the work values of a person answer of the question—"To what extent is the work important for him"? The work values determine—how one feels (pleasure, anxiety, punished or stress) while working. A person develops work values by learning. This learning occurs either through socialization process (including the process of imitation, modelling and conformity) or educational processes. It is a well agreed fact that the education system can be used in order to generate proper work values among people. It has been frequently commented that an education system that does not produce relevant people is not worth its name. Therefore, it is advocated to develop the education system that can instil adequate values (including the work values) along with other essential capabilities and qualities among students.

It is a popular complaint from parents today that they don't feel like their children are engaged in as many work related activities as they were at the same age. This complaint is of universal nature. Parents feel like they were put to work at younger ages and had much more responsibility than their kids do. A 2001 Time/CNN poll stated that 75 per cent of American adults believe that children today do fewer chores than did the children of 10 or 15 years earlier (Retrieved from http//www.myjobchart.com/parenting-tips-blog/2010/03). It indicates that, not only in India but also in America like developed country, it is generally perceived that children today are experiencing less responsibility or are required to do less than children from generations before. When children have little responsibility they have more leisure time. This leaves more room for them to develop other less productive activities to engage in and also it promotes laziness. All of these things can lead to huge detriments for children and their likelihood of succeeding in the future. It is contributing to increase of obesity among children also.

The parents, perturbed with this scenario, are trying to get remedial suggestions from the experts either through appointments or through internets. They want to break the habits of laziness and development of good work habits. The various sites of internets are providing tips to the parents for this purpose (e.g., http//www.myjobchart.com). In facts, these tips are overflooded on the internet and are quite popular among the parents. The essence of most of these tips are related to teaching the children about a variety of direct or indirect benefits of work, including the financial, educational, social, psychological, and physiological benefits. According to these tips, the children must be told about the significance of their works in family or society. All these endeavours would help in creating positive attitudes toward work, consequently leading to the development of healthy work habits and positive work values. The development of positive work values among our children has become very essential today.

The studies have revealed that the work values form particularly during childhood and adolescence. The work values formed during these stages of development are found to be relatively stable over time (Lindsay and Knox, 1984; Johnson, 2002). On the basis of such findings in their studies, the researchers and other academicians have advocated to work for such a curriculum at elementary education system that may inculcate the essential values among the students of these levels. The same is true for the inculcation of work values also. The necessity of reforms in educational system is highlighted in all types of policy declarations in India. Venkataraman (2007) opines that these reforms are needed from elementary level to higher level of education, simultaneously. In any such endeavour, the inculcation of work values among students also should be in the priority list. It should be made part of schemes of value education.

In the context of above theoretical perspectives, a study was planned. However, before presenting the detailed objectives and planning of the study, it seems essential to discuss the issues and review the relevant literature associated with the conceptualization and operationalization of values, works and work values along with the processes and determinants of development of values, specially that of work values. However, in all of these discussions and reviews, the contextual significance of elementary education would always remain in special focus.

Value and Value Development

Liu and Lei (2012) contended that work values are based on human values which provide the epistemological and methodological basement to it. In fact, a person acts not just in service to personal needs, but also out of a broader sense of what is important and meaningful. It can be safely argued that the values are the deepest and most powerful motivators of personal actions. Therefore, the researchers have rightly advocated to develop a clear understanding of nature of general human values before moving forward for any study of work values (Liu and Lei, 2012). That is the reason of presenting a review of literature on the nature, categorization and development of values in this section.

Values are one of our most special achievements as human beings. Human behaviours are governed by values. Values are important component of a person's psyche. So they are inseparable from life of an individual. Values are guiding principles, decisive not only in our day-to-day behaviours but also in critical life situations. Furth (1996), on the basis of the findings from his experiments with infants, deduced that human actions are value driven from the start of the life. Babies playing with one toy rather than the another, or responding to one adult rather than another, are developing fleeting interests and long term preferences while they exercise sense-motor skills. The importance of values in our lives is well elaborated by Scott, Jaffe and Tobe (2004). They have written that "Our values are the deep seated pervasive standards that influence almost every aspect of our lives: our moral judgments, our responses to others, our commitments to personal and organizational goals. We all have belief systems we live by. Our beliefs and value systems are deeply connected. We are motivated and make decisions based on these belief systems and values" (p. 19). It can be further added that the values can act from subconscious and unconscious levels of mind also.

The values that are more or less common among most of the members of a community, form the social values. In fact, an individual does not have a single value, rather he has a system of many values. A value system is a set of consistent values. The value system is described as a learned organization of values and beliefs which helps individuals choose between the given alternatives. The higher the order of significance attached to a given value, the more likely that the value will be activated into action, i.e., behaviour (Mehta, 1994). The value system of an individual is not inborn but is acquired under social conditions. Deb (2008) has rightly stated that the humans are the transmitters of such values. They are generators of new values as well. The value system is passed on across generations, but it is not necessarily accepted by the following generation in exactly the same format or in total. A member of new generation can modify it on the basis of his own learning or even discard some of them and can develop new ones in their places. Thus the process of modifications and development of a value system is a continuous process. This continuity becomes an important system of livelihood of human civilization.

There is a general consensus that values are losing weights in modern days. The current erosions in value system is creating several ailments at individual and societal level. At individual level it is being manifested as self-centredness, an attitude of 'might is right', selfish behaviours along with symptoms of psychological problems; while at societal level it is emerging as the increase in corruption, unethical behaviours, intolerance and ethnic turbulences, etc. Since, the situation has reached to an alarming stage now, therefore, it is being felt that curative interventions are immediately needed. It has happened at universal level and India is not the exception anyway.

Rajiv Gandhi had once commented that only a few paisa of every one rupee allocated for some development programmes reach the real beneficiary in India. The middlemen in the process grab the rest amount. These comments were recognized as the factual statement. While making these remarks, Mr. Gandhi was certainly targeting the problems of corruption and other malfunctions of the system that need eradication. However, the social scientists have opined that along with the lacuna in the system, certain psychological attributes of Indian people, some of which are results of erosions in values, also are equally responsible for such situation (Tiwari, 2003). It seems that there are two types of people in the country. One type of people are those who have become fatalistic, complacent and stagnant due to the influence of religion and traditional belief in *Prarabdh* (Palsane and Lam, 1996). These people do not show the necessary enthusiasm towards the developmental opportunities created by some schemes due to their general mental set to maintain the *status quo*. They express themselves as they are fully contented even in their state of poor quality of life. They accept their poverty because they feel that it is 'Will of God' and it would change when the same God would propose so. This situation gives the middlemen an opportunity to divert the schemes toward their own benefits. The second type of people are those who under the influence of westernization and western education have adopted the western mentality of consumerism (Paranjpe, 2002). These people believe in earning and storing as much as possible. In this process they can go ahead to work for enhancement in their benefits even at the cost of other's heavy losses, further even at the cost of national loss. They are the people who do not care for any of healthy human values while doing this. Thus the two types of mentalities of these two types of people are two extremes, which can be regarded to be responsible for the problem of imbalance that was indicated in the statement of Rajiv Gandhi. On the basis of these arguments, Tiwari (2003) suggested that in order to cure this problem of imbalance, interventions are needed for psychological transformation of Indian people as well as corrective reforms in the system. Since, the values are important parts of one's belief system and psychological makeup that determine his actions, therefore, the interventions should be directed to reform the individual's value system also. It should aim to check the current tendency of erosions in values as well as to inculcate eroded values once again. However, this can be done only through the knowledge about the answers of questions, such as—What is value?, How can the values be classified?, How do the values develop and what are its major determinants?, and In what manner can educational system be used for the purpose of value development?

What is Value?

The concept of value has been changing overtime. Long back it was limited as an economic index for marketing of some physical object.

Later, it was defined as the idealistic and moral components of one's faith and belief system that determine behaviour. In current conceptualization it covers a relatively broader domain. It is now defined as 'a status of human mind, a mental disposition, an attitude or an emotionalized state of mind towards some idea, thing or tradition carrying positive and negative charges within itself. It ...is a result of one's own experience' (Shukla, 2004, p. 5).

In general, the term 'value' denotes for whatever is desired, approved, liked, worthwhile, and valuable. Values are the meaning we attach to things. The term 'value' is a borrowed word from Latin *valere* via old French. The meaning as per the Oxford Dictionary ranges from a sense of estimation, comparison with something, to consideration of the worth, merit, etc. Semantically, the meaning of the word is taken from English *weorden* which is equivalent to worth. (Patil, 2008). Webster's dictionary defines values as 'a principle, standard or quality considered inherently worthwhile or desirable' (Scott, Jaffe and Tobe, 2004). Scott *et al.* further suggested that the root for value is *valor*, which means strength. Values are sources of strength, because they give the people the power to take action. Values are deep and emotional and often difficult to change.

Values are defined differently in different disciplines. It ranges *from* 'a numerical quantity measured or assigned or computed' (in Mathematics) or 'the amount (of money or goods or services) that is considered to be a fair equivalent for something else' (in Commerce) *to* 'an ideal accepted by some individual or group'(in Sociology) or 'the quality (positive or negative) that renders something desirable or valuable' (in Management) or *even to* 'the relative duration of a musical note' (in Music science). In Psychology, values are defined in a broader way. Psychology is the science of behaviour, therefore, it has focused on behavioural aspects of values. So the psychologists, in general, view the values as—the guiding principles, decisive in day-to-day behaviours as also in critical life situations. According to them, values represent the highest and most powerful individual capacity for achievement. As skills direct the use of physical energy, values direct the use of psychological energy of personality (Patil, 2008). In organizational area, values are defined as the principles, the standards, the actions that people in an organization represent, which they consider inherently worthwhile and of the utmost importance (Scott, Jaffe and Tobe, 2004).

Thus it is obvious that as a concept, value is very broad in nature. It consists several constructs. Each discipline defines it emphasizing on the constructs of its interest. It is well elaborated by Rawat (2007), who said—'Generally, value has been taken to mean ideas, general conceptions or orientations towards the world or sometimes simply interests, attitudes, preferences, needs, sentiments and dispositions. But the sociologists use this term in a more precise sense to mean the generalized end which has the connotations of rightness, goodness or inherent desirability. These ends are regarded legitimate and binding by society (p. 93)'. In sociological approach, more emphases remain on collective values. The psychologists focus on behavioural aspects while conceptualizing values. They assume that the values do not only give direction to our behaviours but are also ideals and objectives, proposed to be attained by behaviours. It plays an important role in the integration and fulfilment of man's basic impulses and desires in a stable and consistent manner appropriate for his living.

Scott, Jaffe and Tobe (2004) commented that what is most important to us to accomplish, and to do, at work, in our family and in our personal life and career, can be described in relation to the values we want to achieve. The same was supported by S. Shukla (2004). She stated that when a quality tends to fulfil a human need or evoke feeling of pleasure, it creates 'value'. According to her, this is purely a subjective concept. It differs from situation to situation and even from individual to individual. Some scholars have argued that like attitude, the value also incorporates three types of mental processes; cognitive, affective and conative. The value is realized through cognitive processes. Once a value is realized affective processes dominate over cognition and associate itself with conative (action oriented) tendencies (Shukla, 2004).

Conclusively, it can be said that the values have traditionally been employed in a variety of ways depending on the theoretical and empirical context of different types of studies; and also depending on its objectives (Ravlin and Meglino, 1987). Therefore, the first task of planning any kind of study of some value related issue, would be to clearly specify the procedure of conceptualization and measurement of values. The researcher would have to focus on the nature of values to be studied, how these values affect individuals, and how these values are to be measured. During these exercises, the researcher would have to keep in mind the major objectives of the proposed study. It would be possible only when the researcher is able to comprehend the nature of values and the dynamics of its development.

Categorization of Values

As the above discussed nature of value—as a concept suggests, the values can be many in number. Therefore, the researchers preferred to put them into different categories. The values have been categorized in several ways by different researchers. The classification given by Allport, Vernon and Lindzey (1960); and Rokeach (1973) remained most popular for a long time. There has been a long tradition of studies using the scales develop on the bases of these classifications. Later, Ravlin and Meglino (1987) drew attention towards the limitations of such approaches. They opined that in these approaches, each value of an individual was measured at the expense of his other values. These approaches are based on assumption that the values can be hierarchically organized within an individual. This is not true. More than one value can be equally effective for a particular individual. Therefore, the multiplicities of values should be recognized and they should be studied as an array of values in the individuals.

It was in this context that some researchers classified values in a broader manner. According to a few of them, all values can be classified among the three categories namely; intrinsic, extrinsic and lifestyle values. Intrinsic value has traditionally been thought to lie at the heart of the ethics. Philosophers use a number of terms to refer to such value. The intrinsic value of something is said to be the value that that thing has 'in itself', or 'for its own sake' or 'as such' or 'in its own right' (*Stanford Encyclopaedia of Philosophy*, 2007). Extrinsic value is value that is not intrinsic. Intrinsic values are the intangible rewards, those related to motivation and satisfaction at work on a daily basis. They provide the inner satisfaction and motivation that make people say, 'I love going to work'. The extrinsic values are the tangible rewards or conditions one finds at work, including the physical setting, job titles, benefits and earnings/earning potential. Extrinsic values often trap people into staying at works they do not like. The third, namely lifestyle values are the personal values associated with how and where one wants to live, how one chooses to spend his leisure time. Some values are categorized as instrumental values, as they prove to be instrumental in achieving some other values. They are not the ultimate goals in itself.

S. Shukla (2004) presented an interesting classification of values. She opined that the values are primarily of three types, i.e. physical values, psychic values and economic values. The physical values are expressions of *panch-tatva* in the form of earth *(kchhiti)*, water *(jal)*, fire *(pawak)*, ether *(gagan)*, and air *(samira)* of the whole universe *(Brahmand)*. Psychic values are higher values rooted in volitional nature of individual in the form of thinking, feeling and willing. The economic values are common observations that are convertible or exchangeable.

According to another classification, the values are of two major types—personal values and cultural values. This classification seems to suggest that each individual may possess a system of personal values of unique nature. Cultural values are such values that are largely shared by the majority of the members of a particular culture. The Inglehart-Welzer Cultural map of the world, created by political scientists Ronald Inglehart and Christian Welzer based on the world value survey depicts the cultural values. These values are related to the norms of a culture and the society expects from everyone of his members to have these values. Also types of values include ethical/ moral values, doctrinal/ideological (political, religious) values, social values, and aesthetic values.

Shukla (2004) has reviewed many of the classifications of values. This review reveals that there are several classifications of values depending on different criteria. He reported Karr (1996), who had suggested that most of the traditional and modern values can be categorized across the four *Purusharthas*. In Indian religious-philosophical tradition, the four *Purusharthas*, i.e., *Dharma, Artha, Kama*, and *Moksha* have been regarded to be four supreme ends of one's life. These ends are realized by different kinds of actions that get energy from different types of values. So, the values like moral values, social values or intellectual values help in realizing *Dharma*. Economic values are associated with *Artha*. The aesthetic values or pleasure values or recreational values are instrumental in realization of *Kama*, and religious or spiritual values assist in attempting for *Moksha*. According to Shukla (2004), the values are categorized as lower order and higher order values also. Lower order values are those which are desired for satisfying the biological needs and for seeking pleasure. The higher values are the means to salvation or *Moksha* or spiritual bliss. However, Shukla quickly added that the lower order values should not be underestimated as they play basic roles in gaining higher values.

Thus, it is clear that there are several classifications of values. The researchers can adopt the one, which they feel is more appropriate in the context of objectives of their study. Liu and Lei (2012) have recently argued that more than one type of values combine to form a specific 'value structure' of a particular individual. The different types of values may combine differently to form different 'value structures' for different individuals. Therefore, Liu and Lei (2012) suggested to focus on value-structure of a person or group in the studies. The categorization of values would be very useful in this approach.

Value Development in Children : Review of Relevant Studies

Values go on developing during entire life. However, the speed of development is faster between the periods from childhood to adulthood. After that the values become relatively more stable. Due to the process of value development the span of values in an individual gets expanded with time.

The development of values is largely based on learning processes, for which the family, community, culture and the educational system provide formal or informal platform. Therefore, different characteristics of family, community, culture and the educational system determine the value development. It has been collaborated by the findings of different studies. For example, Rohmetra (2000) obtained the powerful effects of cultural diversity on the variations in values and associated behaviour in India. She had conducted an empirical study to explore the question: How and to what extent do values vary by cultural backgrounds? The results of the study substantiated the determining effects of cultural background on values.

Rogoff, Mistry, Goncu and Mosier (1993), in their survey based study, also found variations in the effects of differences in cultural background of four communities on the process of children's development, including the learning of values. They adopted a macro perspective regarding the composite development of the children in a 'community'. Of course, it included value development also as one of its important components. The community has special significance in the process, as it provides the contexts of skills, values and knowledge, which the toddlers learn and extend during the process of their development. Rogoff *et al.* have very nicely elaborated this significance of community. They mean by community—a group of people having some common local organizations, values and practices.

Further they quote Dewey (1916), who had pointed out that–"*There is more than a verbal tie between the words common, community and communication. People live in a community in virtue of the things which they have in common; and communication is the way in which they come to possess things in common*" (p. 5). Thus the community is not a static notion, rather it is dynamic. It itself passes through continuous evolution.

The development of toddlers in the community at one hand and the continuous evolution of the community at the other, interact with one another to make the entire scenario complex. Noticing this complexity, Rogoff (1990) offered a term "guided participation" to use it in an attempt to keep individual, interpersonal, and cultural processes simultaneously in focus, representing inseparable aspects of whole events in which children and communities develop. The concept provides a perspective on the process by which children develop through their participation in the evolving practices of their community. The concept of guided participation is based on the assumption that children's development occurs 'through their active participation in culturally structured activity with the guidance, support, and challenge of companions who vary in skill and status. ... It stresses guidance—not only in the sense of explicit instruction but also in the sense of development in specific directions that are based on the models of human activity provided by previous generations' (Rogoff *et al.*, 1993, p. 5-6).

Further Rogoff *et al.* planned a study to examine cultural variations in how guided participation occurs—especially the means of shared participation and the balance of responsibility for teaching and learning—as well as in the local goals of development, depending on the values, institutions, technologies, and practices of different communities. They studied four communities which, according to them, represented varied social and economic characteristics that they expected to be associated with differing child-rearing arrangements. The results of their study suggested that there were deep cultural differences in the goals of development, arrangement of childhood activities, and nature of communication between children and their caregivers across the communities. The findings suggested the importance of understanding not only how children learn through instruction that is managed by adults but also how they learn through keen observation and participation in adult activities. It reveals the importance of cultural characteristics of communities as the potent determinants of children's development. This seems to be equally true for the value development among children.

The significant roles of the characteristics of caregivers in shaping the development of children are well depicted by McLoyd (1989, 1990). McLoyd (1989) reviewed the researches on the impact of economic hardship in family due to paternal job and income loss on the children's development. They found support in favour of adverse impact. However, this impact was seen to be indirect in most of the cases. Only in a few cases, it had direct effects on children's development. Generally, the loss of job or income caused behavioural irritations among the parents first, and the behavioural irritations of parents finally resulted with negative effects on physical and socio-emotional development of children.

Later, McLoyd (1990) examined the impact of economic hardship in the family on the children's development in the specific context of black families of America. The basic presumption was that the 'black children in America have always borne a disproportionate share of the burden of poverty and economic decline, and they are at substantially higher risk than white children for experiencing an array of socio-emotional problems' (p. 311). On the basis of review of relevant literature associated with this issue, McLoyd once again drew conclusion that economic hardship adversely affects children's development in part through its impact on the parent's behaviour toward the child. It was more evident in black families.

The rural-urban inhabitation is also found to determine the priorities in the development of values. The studies have revealed that the exposure to urban life determine the development of certain values. For example, the findings of some studies have suggested that the people born and brought up in urban areas have a higher need for personal achievement than others, it results achievement oriented value system among these people (Mehta, 1994).

Education is natural determinant of value development. Education introduces us to worthwhile activities which at first we may not recognize because we have yet to gain the requisite know-how. In schools, as in life, human beings renew their commitment daily in the light of ongoing experiences. Therefore, education is an essential requirement for value development. An integral point of education, is to view the aims of education, content and methodology in terms of value development. In a large number of investigations, the educational socialization has been found to influence the values.

Possibly because of this, concern for adequate value education has been increasingly expressed in recent years, particularly due to the crisis of values that our society is currently experiencing. It is being felt that the ailments of present society can be cured to a great extent through the provision of an effective, meaningful and value-based learning in educational institutions (S. Shukla, 2004). Patil (2008) have stated that–"An important goal of education is to instil within students the universal human values which have stood the test of time and benefited generations, as well as make them aware of their rights as human beings. Cutting across curriculum requisites of various educational boards, the universality of value education and human rights makes them essential components of a child's educational process, an imperative to the ethos of learning".

Prof. Vincent Anigbogu, Director General, Institute for National Transformation (USA) called in his lecture on the theme 'The Role of Schools in National Transformation' to make a total change in attitudes and values in order to achieve the target of transformation of nation. The education sector can be well utilized for the purpose. An education system that does not produce relevant people is not worth its name.

The broader objectives of value education are to inculcate in the children a sense of humanism, a deep concern for the well-being of others and the nation. Value education refers to a programme of planned educational action aimed at the development of value and character. The importance of the human values in education gets lost in globalization, because it only stimulates the educational system by the economic point of view and there's no other reference. Value education is simply a matter of developing appropriate behaviour and habits involving inculcation of certain virtues and habits (Patil, 2008). Also it is said that educationists' objective should be similar to the objectives of an entrepreneur, where the main concern is on production with quality not only with quantity.

The topic of value education is increasingly being popular among the educationists. Now it is being advocated to start such education from elementary education level. For example, Bedley (2003) strongly advocated in favour of cultivating values in middle school kids. He gave eight principles for transmitting values to adolescents, among them the most important and practical principle was to describe them clearly about the expectations of works, needed from children. Sandhu and Mayank Tiwari (2007) presented ten parental posers related to the parents' perception about the development of their children. At least four of these ten posers were associated with the development of work attitudes among children. These posers indirectly suggest the ways of inculcating better understanding of importance of works in family.

Chilana and Dewan (2002) reviewed the educational systems of various institutes including, Sri Sathya Sąi Institute and Dayalbagh Educational Institute and its role in value development among their students. On the basis of this review, they suggested that in order to develop values, it would be of special significance for the schools to take care of daily routine of the students. Also, the yearly events, such as summer courses can be strategically planned. The schools should utilize its all the ingredients like curriculum, methodology, teacher training, physical education, athletics, drama, adventure activities, debates and other co-curricular activities to teach progressive values among students. The focus should be to combine academic excellence with these values. The values should be more lived than talked about.

The curriculum and teachers are two important components of any educational system. Therefore, both have major roles in value education. The educational planners, thinkers and researchers—all have agreement at this point. These people opine that any educational reform (with the intention of value development or other types of progressive development) would necessarily require appropriate modifications in curriculum and effective teachers' training.

Unfortunately, the Indian education system has not been able to recognize the necessity of above suggested modifications. It is still relying on traditional practices. That is why, its significance in a development oriented nation is being questioned now. The educational system in India has been frequently criticized for its emphasis on 'rote learning'. It encourages students to rote the 'right answers' (exactly the same as given in books, one can say it 'the bookish answer') of the questions that are likely to be asked in examinations. It gives students only theoretical knowledge. In this system, the students are not encouraged to go in some field in order to gain practical knowledge by learning through their 'works'. In India, one, on the basis of his theoretical knowledge, can get an appointment of an engineer without having any practical knowledge of machines or industrial working. Certainly it is not a suitable condition for generation of adequate work values among students. Amit Mitra—the General Secretary of FICCI (2007), after comparing Indian educational system with American educational system has concluded that our system teaches the students 'to give answers', whereas American system teaches 'to raise questions'. Therefore, the students of our country depend heavily on the books or other printed matters in seeking the answers. In contrast to it, American students develop a critical approach and learn not only through books but through practical or 'works' in the related fields also. Mitra further claimed that those students of our country, who visit abroad and learn the habits of raising questions there, perform remarkably well. These contentions suggest that the educational system needs transformation in our country. Venkataraman (2007) opines that such transformation should be from elementary level to higher level of education, simultaneously. In any such endeavour, the inculcation of work values among students also should be in the priority list. It should be made part of schemes of value education.

The necessity of reforms in educational system is highlighted in all types of policy declarations in India. The National Education Policy (1986) declares that the growing concern over the erosion of essential values and increasing cynicism in society has brought to focus the need for readjustment in the curriculum in order to make the education a forceful tool for the cultivation of social and moral values. Curriculum should be based on the needs of the individual and also of society. It should have clear vision regarding objectives of education. So the National Curriculum Framework for School Education 2000 observed that the school curriculum necessarily should have to contain components that communicate essential values in their totality (Patil, 2008). The importance of curriculum was shown through their study by Silcock and Wyness (2000). These researchers found in their study of 10 to 11 years old school students that their interest in different subjects (such as music, gymnastic or art) was affected by the biases build in the curriculum of the subjects. Thus the results suggested that curricular organization or curricular management play major role in choosing the study area of interest.

The teachers also have great role in value education. They are always expected to instil appropriate values among their students (Nnaike, 2008). Similar voice was raised here in India by Cynthia Pandian, the Vice-Chancellor of the M.S. University, Tirunelveli. She appealed teachers to teach human values among students. She advised to curriculum framers to be committed to promoting a vibrant and competencies-development oriented academic activities. According to her, 'one of the key activities in this challenging process is restructuring curricula, which should be employment related, personality development related, work ethics, standards and values related, at the same time enabling students to perform well in various States and national level competitive examinations'. Also, the teachers should be trained accordingly because the teacher is not only an individual but also a person who is able to change the psyche of an institution, students and society (Pandian, 2005).

Work and Work Value

Work is an integral part of human life. Gupta (2002) has rightly said that be it a man or a nation, work and only work is key to its success. All types of growths—physical or intellectual—depend upon the works. Not only is this, according to Gupta, the civilization of a society is recognized by work habits of its inhabitants. The recognition of Japan, as a nation of hard working people is an appropriate example of the same. Freud (1930) was of the view according to which 'work is a person's strongest tie to reality'. Jahoda (1981) endorsed this notion of Freud and emphasized the relevance of work in human life suggesting that features of the work provide links to reality which prevents people becoming overwhelmed by fantasy and emotion, and thus connect them to the practical goals in the life.

However, despite all these importance of 'work' it is not easy to understand—what the word 'work' exactly means. This is because people have feelings of ambivalence toward work. In a survey, a group of employed persons were asked a direct question: What makes the difference between something you would call 'work' and something you would call 'not work'? Most of them answered this question saying that; 'if an activity was enjoyable in itself, it was not work'. And yet the same people, who defined work in this fashion, also said that they would like to go on working even if they did not make money by doing it (Khan, 1981). Thus the work is liked and disliked simultaneously. This confusion in people's perception of work makes it difficult to define the 'work' as a concept.

What is Work?

There is a consensus that to define 'work' in few words is very difficult as it gets expressed in several form; for example, as a duty, or as a role associated with some post, or as a hobby, or as an order-obedience, or as an entertaining and pleasure seeking behaviour, etc. Its domain functionally overlaps with several processes. Also, the conceptualization of work has taken different form at different phases of time. It also made difficult to define the concept of work in precise manner. Rodgers (1980) presented the historical review of changes in conception of 'work' during different time phases of nineteenth and early twentieth century in America. According to his opinion, work was based on fear induced obedience before 1830s. After 1830, a strikingly different conception of work—marked not by obedience but by self-control, and induced not through fear but through the systematic inculcation of habits came forward. Finally at the turn of nineteenth century, a third pattern of essential meaning of work emerged, which was injected by a new explicit insistence on conformity into child life. It highlighted the impacts of social factors. Every time the changes in conception of work produced the challenges before the schooling system and necessitated adequate transformation in it also. Although the review by Rodgers was in American contexts, but it can be universalize to say that in every society/nation, the conception of work changes with time and the society/nation should have the skills to modify its schooling system—including curriculum, accordingly.

Mirowsky (2011) also have adopted a historical approach. He summarized the Western philosophical views of work from ancient to modern times. According to him, the western philosophical and scientific traditions often have viewed human work as 'inherently onerous, wearisome, and degrading'. He points out that Adam Smith, writing in the eighteenth century, saw work as the toil and trouble that is the real price humans pay for everything they need or want. Mirowsky further presented the opinion of Karl Marx, expressed in the nineteenth century. Karl Marx had considered wage labour alienating, but had seen the possibility of self-expressive work. During the end of the twentieth century Dupré and Gagnier, the well known philosophers and critic writers, opined that work could be self-fulfilling, but only for an elite minority. Mirowsky conducted an empirical study also. He statistically analyzed the data drawn from a 1995 U.S. survey. The analysis suggested that work, in general, is recognized to be more self-fulfilling than onerous, alienating, or degrading in modern America.

Work is a pleasure or a curse—the debate on this issue has a long history. However, it is generally accepted that it largely depends on the attitude of the person. If one enjoys the work, it is a pleasure that consequently makes one's life a joy. At the other hand if the work is regarded to be a hard and tough duty, life is agonized. Carlyle, in his famous classic book *Past and Present*, has rightly pointed out—"Blessed is he who has found his work; let him ask no other blessedness". It suggests that if you get some meaningful and useful work to do, do not ask for other boon. Gupta (2002) noted that '....everyone has got his own work ethos. This ethos is originated from his own culture and cultural values. That is why work ethos among people of different cultures differs from nation to nation and from time to time'. He further commented that 'work itself is a great value, but this great value never stands alone. It has its associates which include devotion, honesty, sincerity, humaneness and discipline, etc.' With these opinions, Gupta emphasized on developing school atmosphere more congenial for inculcation of various values among the students. It would create positive work-attitudes among them. Thus they would be able to take work as a pleasure not as a curse. In fact, as Underwood (1965) has stated, work is vitally dependent upon motivation. Depending on intensity of motivation, work may bring frustration or conflict or even pleasure at different occasions.

There have been many discussions on the distinctions between 'work' and 'leisure'. The review of these discussions seems to be useful in understanding the meaning of work.

White (1978) produced his opinions on the distinction between 'work' and 'leisure' (presented as the 'reply to the critical comments by T.H. Hull' on the article of Nag, White and Peet, 1978). According to his views, the traditional Victorian notion—that work is what you would prefer someone else to do, while leisure activity is what you would prefer to do yourself even if another is willing to take your place, is wrong. Also it is not always true that what is enjoyable can not be considered work. White feels that the work can be distinguished from leisure on the basis of 'relevance of the output of the activity'. Drenth, P.J.D., Thierry, H., Willems, P.J. and de Wolff, C.J. (1984) underlined that leisure does not mean 'to do nothing'. According to them 'Leisure' (derived from French 'loisir'; Latin 'lic'ere') means 'being permitted to'(The American Heritage Dictionary of the English Language). This implies that the emphasis is on having opportunity being able to choose, not on what one need not to do (e.g., not working) p. 618. Parker and Smith (1976) adopted rather a different approach on the distinction between work and leisure. They used the time duration of 'work' and said it 'the working time'. Then after they distinguished it from the 'remaining or spare time'. Further, they classified the remaining or spare time under four broad categories, which are:

- *Work related time*: Commuting time, preparation of work, etc.
- *Existence time*: Meals, sleep, etc.
- *Semi-leisure*: Activities of an obligatory nature, such as walking the dog, paying calls, etc.
- *Leisure*: Time to be spent at liberty.

Thus it is clear that 'leisure' does not mean 'to do nothing'. Rather it indicates some work, which is done without any type of compulsion. The absence of compulsion makes such work 'a mean of enjoyment' and has effect of being a reward.

Work is important in the lives of individuals for several reasons. It provides various types of extrinsic and intrinsic rewards. From a psychological standpoint, it can be an important source of identity, self-esteem, and self-actualization. It can provide a sense of purpose and worthwhileness by clarifying his or her value to society. Marini, Pi-Ling, Erica and Ann (1996) have distinguished among seven types of work rewards. These rewards are; extrinsic rewards, security, intrinsic rewards, influence, altruistic rewards, social rewards, and leisure. The 'extrinsic rewards include instrumental and status-attainment rewards such as income, advancement opportunities and prestige. Security refers to work stability. Intrinsic rewards reflect the inherent interest of works, the learning potential and the opportunity to be creative. Influence, though often combined with intrinsic rewards, refers to the opportunity to exercise power through involvement in decision-making and challenging work. Altruistic rewards are derived from doing things for others, such as directly helping others or making a contribution to society. Social rewards are interpersonal and include positive relations with coworkers, the opportunity to make friends, and working with people. Finally, leisure refers to the opportunity for free time, vacation, and freedom from supervision' (Quoted by Johnson, 2002).

Warr (1984) have summarized the principal material and psychological benefits derived from a job. Although he was referring here the job associated with employment of an individual, but his contentions were safely generalizable for all types of works. The benefits are as given below:

1. *Money*: Many of the jobs, particularly the paid jobs provide money which is essential for livelihood of people.
2. *Raised activity levels*: The opportunity to work provides outlets for physical and mental energy, and may permit the exercise and development of personal skills. One basis of mental health is the establishment and attainment of realistic goals, and it is partly through a work that goals may be defined and achieved.
3. *Variety*: The engagement in some kind of work permits access to facilities, equipment and behaviours which are not otherwise available.
4. *Temporal structure*: The occupational tasks or some other types of routinized works divide one's time span into segments each with its own built—in structure and goals. However, for most people, the introduction of greater temporal structure into their lives (as the benefit of paid work), is not recognized unless it is lost.
5. *Social contacts*: Many of the works, including the paid jobs give access through encounters with other people to a range of new ideas and shared experiences. Social support from colleagues may be available to help with current problems in everyday living. Work activities can contribute to group goal achievement and a sense of being valued by coworkers.
6. *Personal identity*: The works and associated roles can contribute in important ways to personal identity and self perceptions.

An overview of these benefits makes it clear that the works are beneficial from a variety of points of view including the financial, psychological, social and individual point of views. The work is instrumental in attaining at least five Ps- 'Pleasure', 'Paisa', 'Prosperity', 'Prestige' and 'Power'.

Apart from the rewards, in certain situation the work however, can also be a source of frustration, boredom, and feeling of meaninglessness (Steers and Porter, 1979). Perhaps this is the reason of ambivalent attitudes towards work among people. At the one hand people show aversion towards work but at the same time, they are largely in agreement with the notion of 'work hard'. In Indian philosophy, four types of *Purusharthas* are described, as the goals for an individual at various stages of his life. The *Purusharthas* are; *Dharma, Artha, Kama,* and *Moksha.* These *Purusharthas* can be realized only by specific types of 'works' prescribed for each of them.

Significance of Children's Work

Apart from the description of conceptualization of 'work' in general, several researchers have expressed their views on children's works and its significance in family, society and community. There has been a general consensus that the children's work has both psychological and sociological implications. Therefore, the scholars of various disciplines have taken deep interests in the issues associated with the children's work and its significance. However, the psychologists had always a lead in researching this area. Since, it was felt that the development of nice work habits influences the complete psychological development of the child as an individual, children's work or lack of it, soon became a major concern for psychologists. The sociologists started late, therefore, the sociological researches on children's work are available only in a few number.

White and Brinkerhoff (1981) have critically analyzed some of the opinions about significance and meaning of children's works in the family. They argue that children's work has been a sight light rather than a focus of research, therefore, there is little accurate descriptive data on this issue. There has not been any systematic consideration of the meaning of children's work for family and its interactions with other organizations. In this context, a little literature is available in this area that too contains contrasting viewpoints. According to first viewpoint, the primary obligation of the children is to enjoy the childhood, so they should not be expected to work hard in the home or outside home except in schools. If in any case, the children do such works, it inhibits them from achieving in schools or social lives (Roy, 1961). The second viewpoint suggested that the children, who do some kind of household chores, quickly develop the sense of responsibility, service and self control that ultimately helps them in socialization with adult roles (Kohlberg, 1964). In an attempt to investigate the relationship between children's work at household and their strive for excellence, McClellan (1961) conducted an empirical study and found inverse relationship between the two.

However, Smith (1969) did not find such relationship in his study. The studies by Nye and Haffman (1974) also suggested that children's works in home have no adverse consequences on children's social life. In fact, the major findings of the study of Nye and Haffman were in support of second viewpoint.

The second viewpoint was supported by some other researchers also. For example, Staff and Mortmer (2007) analyzed the data from the Youth Development Study of adolescents and found that moderate work coupled with school appears to especially facilitate the educational attainment of low promise youths. He concluded that steady part time work during high school proved especially conducive to human capital development. It gave the adolescents a training of time management that positively influenced higher educational attainment. Mortimer, Pimentel, Ryu, Nash, and Lee (1996) examined the interrelations of work experiences and occupational values in a panel of 1,000 adolescents, who were engaged in some kind of part time works. They found that the opportunity to learn useful skills at work was a consistent positive influence on increasingly stable intrinsic and extrinsic value dimensions among adolescents. They had planned their study with the assumption that because adolescence is a crucially important period for the formation of vocational interests and identity, it is reasonable to suppose that work experience would have a significant formative influence on adolescents' thinking about the potential rewards to be obtained from work. They noted several types of consistent positive effects of the working. According to them, the working at adolescence level enhanced different types of competence. It provided the adolescents opportunity to learn skills that are useful in the future, on the intrinsic value dimension. Also, they learn how to accept responsibility, get along with people, be on time, manage money, and follow directions. They come to view the intrinsic benefits of work. It is certainly more important. Loughlin and Barling (1998), on the basis of the findings of their study, suggested that only intensive work during high school exerts negative effects for teenagers.

Goldstein and Oldham (1979) also worked on the issue of children's work and its role in their development. However, they adopted a new approach and developed a new area, which was regarded as the third area of research regarding children and work. This area focused on children's socialization with adult work roles. They concluded that the children do work themselves and that their own experiences, as well as, other influences around them, may affect their work socialization.

More particularly, these experiences and influences have great impact on children's socialization with adult work roles. Rodgers (1980) regarded it important from the 'development of character' point of view among children. According to him, it results obedience through self controlled work habits, not through any kind of fear.

Strong, Silver and Robinson (1995) have forcefully contended that the students want and need work that enables them to demonstrate and improve their sense of themselves as competent and successful human beings. These sentiments of the students need to be supported in classrooms. How can these drives be cultivated in classrooms? In an attempt to answer this question Strong and his associates worked on a research project and developed a formula of 'SCORE' on the basis of findings of this project. In this formula, the first letter 'S' denoted success, 'C' curiosity, 'O' originality, and 'R' relationships. They contended that the students, who were engaged in their works, are driven by these four essential goals—success, curiosity, originality and satisfying relationship. Each of these goals satisfies a particular human need. Success satisfies the need for mastery, curiosity the need for understanding, originality the need for self-expression and relationship the need for involvement with others. The four goals form the acronym for a model of student engagement. Under the right classroom conditions and at the right level for each student, they can build the motivation and Energy (the initial of which, i.e., 'E' completed the acronym of 'SCORE') that is essential for a complete and productive life. These goals can provide students with the energy to deal constructively with the complexity, confusion, repetition and ambiguities of life.

White and Brinkerhoff (1981) interviewed parents of the children also, with an objective to understand the parents' opinions about the children's works. They found that the parents themselves believe that assigning works to children is always beneficial on various criteria. It helps in responsibility sharing and character formation. Also, by doing works children learn skills, help the family and make the bonds among family members stronger. White and Brinkerhoff, in the same study, further found that the meaning of children's works depend on several contextual variables associated with family characteristics and that of the children. It suggested the possibilities of different work values in different types of family frameworks. The variations of meaning of work create different types of family theme, which ultimately determine the work values prevalent in a family.

Nag, White and Peet (1978) took an anthropological approach in their study of work of children and its values in Javanese and Nepalese peasant families. They found strong gender differences on the basis of work done by children in these families. Girls were found working more in comparison to boys. Work input by these children was found to increase with the age, but the sharp increase occurred during the age range of 12 years to 15 years. (Interestingly, this is the age range during which the children study at Junior High School level in India. The study, reported in the present dissertation was concerned with the work values at this very level). Nag, White and Peet highlighted the economic values of children's work also.

The above review of researches and the academic works based on theoretical analyses makes it apparent that the works of children have significance from several angles. The same is recognized by the parents, teachers and even by the laymen of the society. In the context of this recognition of significance of children's works, it is unfortunate to note the popular complaint from parents today that they don't feel like their children are engaged in as many work related activities as they were at the same age. So they are worried. The parents want their children to be responsible, helpful, and a contributing member of the family and society. Therefore, they are seeking advices from all possible sources to create work orientations among their children. The internet websites are flooded with the questions and answers related to curiosities about the ways of inculcation of interests in works among children. Some of the advices are summarily presented below, which can be of use for the parents (Retrived from; *http// www.mychart.com/parenting-tips-blog/2010/03*; Category: Advice for Parents Struggling to get Children to Work).

1. It is vital to give child responsibilities. When children have little responsibility they have more leisure time. This leaves more room for them to develop other, less productive (sometimes even destructive) activities to engage in and also promotes laziness. Giving responsibility to the child should start as early as possible because if the start is late, it would have to face a habit of laziness which would have developed in him before this start. To break the habit of laziness is found to be very difficult.
2. It is very important to offer some kind of incentives for your children to do work. Incentives are the necessary part of

motivation. But the researchers have cautioned against too frequentative use of financial (as the money) incentives. It would develop an attitude in child to work only when he is 'bribed' for it. The parents need to understand that the incentives are of many types. Praise, recognition and the intrinsic attributes of works may also act as incentives. These incentives, when effectively used, result with the development of more positive work values among children. Researchers have also suggested that incentives should be given only for completed work. In only some exceptional cases, partially-completed works can be rewarded. It would teach the child not to leave his work uncompleted.

3. The children want to feel useful to their parents. The parents need to let them know that they really NEED their help (even if they really don't). Let the children see the value they provide in the home by giving them chores they alone can be responsible for, and reward them accordingly.
4. It is important that the parents do not just simply ask their children what they "have" to do. This is often met with a negative response and it is less likely that they will do what they have been told. If anyhow they do it, they would not enjoy the work and they would give a half hearted effort and not take interests in the value of the job that they could have otherwise. As far as possible, the parents should associate themselves with the work—being done by the child. They should keep communication open with the child to share his experiences in the work. They should teach the child "how" to work and how to use different tools. Teaching children simple life skills will be a benefit to them and will help them understand the value of being able to accomplish tasks by themselves.
5. Sometimes the child needs a little extra assistance in his struggle to complete his list of chores. The parents or some other members of the family should be available to them for any such type of help, but in no condition, the helpers should take into their hands the child's work to complete (even the 'homeworks').
6. The parents should recognize that all the children do not have similar capabilities. Each child varies in maturity level. The boys and girls develop different skills at different stages.

Therefore, they should not compare the children with each other on the basis of work done by them. Each child is different. He should be expected to perform as per his abilities only. Just because the elder child had worked well in the age of the younger child, the younger child should not be given similar chores. The assignment of chores to the children beyond their maturity or ability would have negative impact on their development.

7. The parents should learn to challenge their children. They should hold children accountable for the work they do. In this condition, they would feel a greater sense of self-worth as they are provided with opportunities to prove their competence.
8. The attempts should be directed to develop a good work-habit in the child. It is said that if something is done for 21 days, it gets turned to be 'a habit'. The neurophysiologists have suggested that when one does something, his brain makes connections that create pathways for neurological activities. When one routinely performs the same actions, his brain learns this pattern of behaviour and sets up a pathway of permanent nature. This pathway becomes the basis of a habit. The parents, trying to develop good work habit in the child, should present themselves as the role-model before the child. The researchers have opined that the best way to teach children good habits is by setting a good example. Setting good habits for kids and instilling values in the children go hand in hand. Good habits for kids will ensure that the child grows up to be a loving and caring person who is self-disciplined and thus will succeed in life.

Work Value: General Conceptualization

The work is of various types; such as physical, mental, clerical, administrative, etc. People have different attitudes towards these types of works. This seems to hold true universally. Singh (1999) has noted, '*People attach different meanings and values to their work. Some regard it as punishment, hardship or an unpleasant obligation. Some it as a duty to fulfil one's predestined calling. Still for others it as a central aspect of their lives. Why some people work harder than others? Partial explanation may be given by their work values'(p. 92)*.

Work is the effort or activity of an individual that is undertaken for the purpose of providing goods and services of value to others and that is also considered by the individual to be work. Before a person learns about a particular job, he or she learns how to feel and thinks about work. In other words, a person develops work values first. In this context the work values have relevance to talk about. The way a person thinks about the works, the way he performs it and the level of his identification with works—all combine to indicate the work values of that very person. Thus the work values are complex in nature. They shape the lifestyle of people and have impact on the society. Therefore, it is simultaneously personal as well as social. It has religious and moral/ethical components too.

The work values determine how one feels (pleasure/anxiety/stress) while working. Also, it determines one's preferences for some specific types of works. It can be said that the link between individuals and their work is one of the reciprocity. People tend to either find work that matches their orientation or try to change the content of their work so that it more closely matches their personality. For instance, a worker valuing autonomy might take steps to increase his freedom from direct supervision. It has been found that the person who deals with complex matters on the job is more flexible and tolerant off the job; jobs that are repetitive and challenging are linked to conformist orientation. At the same time, people who are flexible and tolerant tend to seek more complex jobs, and those who are conformist tend to seek less challenging jobs. Sometimes, the right match between one's personality and liking for the work is seen to make a person 'workaholic'. Thus the work values can be considered to have great impact on the individual.

Work value has been extensively studied in the areas of Industrial and Organizational Behaviour. The focus of study reported in this book was on the work values in the specific context of children. However, the acquaintance about works done in the industrial and organizational areas would be certainly helpful in providing sound bases for the study.

In the areas of Industrial and Organizational Behaviour the 'work' has been defined as the specific roles associated with some position in the organization. Therefore, the basic question that is primarily addressed in those areas is: How does an incumbent of a post value his roles in the organization? But in the studies of work values in other areas are based on conceptualization of 'work' in a generalizable and broader fashion. Whatever, we do or whenever we invest our physical or mental energy, we are engaged in some sort of work. Here, the work is not limited to one's profession. Be it home or club or office, everywhere we do some kind of work. In Hindi there are two words, *Kaam* and *Aram*. When we are not in a state of *Aram*, we are at some *Kaam*. Such *Kaam* is work here. When we speak high for work orientations or workaholism of Japanese people we intend to suggest that they work hard in every field of their lives, not only in their organization.

Some great thinkers have argued that a living human being always works. If the person is looking like doing nothing, then too he is involved in this or that type of work. While sitting idle at the chair he might be engaged in shaking his legs, or in the room, he may be seen walking from this corner to that corner or moving towards window of his room to look outside. Several similar examples can be observed in our daily life, which confirm that at no moment one is without work. In fact, every individual possesses 'a mind' that can not be stopped. Therefore, the individual is bound to be engaged in some work either consciously or unconsciously (Sir Shree, 2011). Also, each piece of work is certainly followed by some sort of consequence. Now if to work is essential and the consequence of it is inevitable, then why should one not try to engage in such works, which might produce consequences—beneficial not only for himself, but for whole community, society or nation. This can be treated to be the core issue of work value.

There has been a growing interest in recent years in the study of value system in general and of work values specifically. The concept of work values, however, has been the subject of controversy in the literature (Sagy, 1997). Liu and Lei (2012) have noted that in the past 30 years, many literatures have focused on researches of the work values. However, most of these were stranded on the facet of empirical research. They did not discuss it in depth or theoretically analyze the connotation of work values. Such analyses are necessarily needed in order to comprehend the real nature of work values.

As has been indicated earlier, the work values have been more often represented in broader fashion. It is operationalized either as motivational constructs or work ethics or personality or self-concept at different occasions. Why some people work harder than others? Partial explanation may be given through their work values (Singh, 1999). Furthermore, a person's values answer the question—"what is important to me"? In this sense the work values of a person answer the question—"To what extent is the work important for him"? The work values determine—how one feels (pleasure, anxiety, punished or stress) while working. A person develops work values by learning. This learning occurs either through socialization process (including the process of imitation, modelling and conformity) or educational processes. Dawis (2001) defines work values as—what a person wants out of work in general and also which components of a job are important to their work satisfaction. According to Johnson (2002), work values are defined by the importance attached to various rewards of working. Extending support to the approach to link work values with the rewards, Marini *et al.* (1996) operationalized seven domains of work values on the basis of his classification of work rewards. As has been mentioned earlier, Marini *et al.* have discussed seven types of work rewards as; extrinsic rewards, security, intrinsic rewards, influence, altruistic rewards, social rewards, and leisure. Monica (2005) defined work values as the beliefs about the desirability of various work features and are usually applied by referencing potential rewards derived from working (e.g., pay, prestige, or opportunity to learn). This is a short, simple and easily understandable definition, and focuses more on attributes of works. Yu and Li (2003) produced a definition of work values, which is more inclusive and is based on a 'synthesis' perspective. This definition has adopted a cognitive perspective. According to this definition, '*work values are an information system with stability, generalization and dynamic functions which are in terms of the needs of people for work, work behaviour and work results, are reflected general values in career life, are the estimation for social and occupational needs by individuals' (p. 49)*. It substantiates the assumption of complexity of the concept of work value.

Work values are important for several reasons. First, by assigning levels of importance to the various components of the work, the individual may determine the range of jobs that he or she will perform effectively or ineffectively. A direct link may exist between the level of perceived importance and the level of actual performance. Achievement by an individual in any field of activity depends on the level of skill, the person has acquired. It also depends on the attitudes, understanding, decisiveness and values with which the individual acts. The researches have revealed that the work values of the person determine the attitude of person towards the work, he is supposed to do.

Most of the times the work has instrumental value, because one can achieve prestige, or power like psychological rewards at one hand and money or some other type of physical rewards at the other, only through the work. In some situations, this instrumentality poses threats to the implication of work. Due to this instrumentality, one pays more attention to the importance of rewards and also to the probability of success in achieving it while working, rather than to work with his unquestionable commitment. The two factors—'satisfiers' and 'motivators' presented in 'Two-factor Theory of Work Motivation' by Herzberg (1966), seem to provide basements for two different categories of work values. These factors support the instrumentality of works also.

In developing countries like India, where there is scarcity of many rewards/resources (J.B.P. Sinha, 1990), the association between the 'work' and the 'expected outcome' is always unpredictable. This unpredictable instrumentality may affect the work values of people adversely. However, a unique approach to the 'work', available in Indian religious-philosophical tradition, has capacity to moderate such adverse effects. This approach to the 'work' has been advanced through the notion of '*Nishkam Karma*', that is 'the work done without having overt attachment to some rewards'. *Nishkam Karma Yoga*, as has been preached more elaborately in *Srimad Bhagwad Gita*, suggests that everyone should perform his works with his full dedication and should pay little attention to the rewards. Such work would certainly result with some kind of reward; either just after the completion of work, or sometimes in future. It is not only order of Almighty God (*Vidhi Ka Vidhan*), but also is law of nature. However, it is quite possible that the person—engaged in work, be unable to identify the reward obtained. Since, the *Nishkam Karma Yoga* is based on 'birth-rebirth theory' therefore, it is preached that if anyhow, the reward is not obtained in the present life, it will be accumulated as a part of *Prarabdh* for next life after rebirth. Once this belief is germinated in an individual, he would be soon able to develop equivalence of feelings in situations of success and failure. Therefore, he would not be over pleased in success, or over drowned on failure. It would positively associate with healthy work attitudes.

This approach to work, i.e., the *Nishkam Karma* approach is found associated with better mental health also. As has been indicated earlier, the person having the instrumental approach to work, becomes more concerned for success in the work and for the consequent rewards.

Therefore, any kind of failure makes him anxious. It may result frustration, stress or other types of mental upsets at different occasions. Contrast to it, in *Nishkam Karma* approach, the equivalence of feelings in both success and failure conditions, protects the person from these symptoms. The studies on *Anasakti* (Non-attachment) have obtained results supporting this contention (Pandey and Naidu, 1992). These results also supported the discourse of Swami Chinmayanand who described the *Bhagawad Gita* as the best manual for sound mental health.

Thus it appears that the *Nishkam Karma* approach to work should be highlighted, as it would not only improve mental health of our people, also it would check the tendencies of corruption and other malpractices that have developed among us due to our lust of material rewards. Some people raise question on the significance of this approach in this materialistic era. Responding to this question, Tiwari (2000) argued that—'*to act with a sense of non-attachment is not necessarily a religious requirement. Rather it is a skill which has positive motivational implications (p. 159)*'. This skill should be developed and nurtured as a part of work values in our country. The educational system can be used for this purpose also. This perspective on work and work values, if proposed scientifically, can get international recognition and may prove to be an important and unique contribution of Indian understanding in this area.

A number of researches on work values have been conducted by Indian researchers also. Most of these researches are conducted in industrial and organizational fields. The results of these studies have indicated certain points that are more relevant in Indian context. As indicated earlier in India also, work values do occupy a place in the studies of organizational behaviour, and the same has attracted limited attention in the sphere of education in general and school education in particular. In the researches conducted in organizations, work values have been found to significantly contribute to organizational output variables (e.g., Kaur and Singh, 2000). Many researchers have noted changes in work values in our country after Independence. Ganesh (1982) wrote that work, as a concept has not been internalized in India. Sinha (1990) supported this by saying that 'work' is not intrinsically valued in our country. In Indian organizations the employees do not derive any satisfaction from their work. They always try to maximize their personal gains in physical terms. Therefore, Sinha (1994) suggested building a new work culture, which he named as Synergetic Work Culture. In this work culture the work itself, should be established as a Meta value. It should be developed as a norm, duty and disposition. Whenever, it would happen the work is likely to turn into a drive, i.e., self-propelled and self-satisfying activity.

The famous communist leader Sri Chaturanan Mishra (1994) went beyond his political ideology while suggesting improvement in work values among workers. He opined that the various schemes of welfare of working class have not improved the level of their work due to lack of a proper work culture. A work culture of national order should be developed in the country but while doing this we should not copy other countries. There must be a national awareness that no nation can be built without a proper work culture, and also no nation should try to copy work culture of some other country.

Tan and Khoo (2002) have found that in India, significant role is played by religious beliefs and social factors in the workforce's perception of work. Suar (1992) observed that there are a large number of work values in India and they can be arranged hierarchically. In his study he compared the work values of managers with that of workers. It was found that the managers put more emphasis on work values of self-actualization, social concern and self-expression than other values. These values can be said to be of higher order. The workers were found to care more for materialistic values than for other values in work. They outscore the managers on these values. These are the values of relatively lower order. The manager and workers both put almost equal emphasis on and seek equal satisfaction with sociopsychological values of achievement and human relations in work. Suar categorized these values as of middle order. On the basis of above overview of literature, two conclusions can be drawn, particularly for Indian context:

1. Work values are of several types. They can be organized hierarchically.
2. The existing work values need to integrate moral and ethical concerns with them.

Work Value and its Inculcation in the Specific Context of Children: Overview of Literature and Studies

The findings of studies and conclusions of reviews of relevant literature on work and work values, available in industrial and organizational academic fields have been attempted to extend and generalize under certain possible conditions, in order to understand the nature of work values in the specific context of children. However, it always needed precautions and preciseness. Any such extension or generalization would be fair only if the findings of the studies on work values and models—developed on the basis of these studies in industrial and organizational academic fields—are empirically authenticated focusing children's works and work values. This fact drew attention of many researchers and these researchers conducted a number of studies in this area. They utilized the knowledge available in industrial and organizational fields to develop relevant hunches for their studies.

The research works, done in the specific areas of children's works and work values, have adopted analytical and empirical—both the approaches. The overview of such researches has yielded many meaningful and attention seeking findings. Some of them are discussed in following points. However, at the outset, it should be clarified that most of the studies of work values of children had focused on its consequences for the occupational values as well. Therefore, there may appear some synonymy between them.

1. There are a number of studies on children's works and work values, which have attempted to identify the types and factors of children's work values. Some scales for measuring children's work values are developed on the basis of these types and factors. Some scales of children's work values have been developed by researchers on the basis of different factors of work values that were specifically relevant in the context of children. For example, The Ohio Work Values Inventory (OWVI) is a 77-item inventory developed by Hales and Fenner (1973, 1975) to measure specifically the work values of elementary school children. The OWVI has been used on a wide range of elementary school children. The OWVI yields scores on 11 scales (7 items per scale): (a) Altruism (helping others), (b) Object Orientation (making or handling things), (c) Job Security (having steady work), (d) Control (being in charge of others), (e) Self-Realization (using one's skills and talents), (0) Independence (being one's own boss), (g) Money (being paid well), (h) Task Satisfaction (liking the tasks one does), (i) Solitude (not working closely with others), (j) Ideas-data (using ideas or facts), (k) Prestige (being known for one's

work). Weisgram (2006) developed a scale for his study that consisted 16 items measuring the endorsement of four gender-typed values: (a) altruism, (b) family, (c) money, and (d) power.

Marini Pi-Ling, Erica and Ann (1996) developed a scale to assess seven domains of work values, based on their distinction among seven types of work rewards as extrinsic rewards, security, intrinsic rewards, influence, altruistic rewards, social rewards, and leisure; and used this scale to enquire into the pattern of changes in these domains of work values during the development from adolescent to adulthood.

Wollack, Goodale, Wijting and Smith (1971) constructed a set of scales measuring several areas of work values. It was named as 'Survey of Work Values (SWV)'. It was different from other scales of work values in the sense that it was directed towards separate areas of work values and also was limited to the construct of secularized Protestant Ethic. The Protestant Ethic presents the man's industriousness as the most crucial aspect of work values, which proves to be beneficial not only for a specific job but for all sorts of works, in general. Thus it assesses work values as the index of a person's attitudes towards any kind of work. It differs from the job satisfaction, which represents an attitude towards one's own job.

Survey of Work Value (SWV) based on Protestant Ethic deals with the intrinsic aspects of work; that is, work as its own reward. Here, work is to be valued because it represents the best use of a man's time, not merely because it is instrumental to the attainment of external rewards. These intrinsic aspects are: pride in work itself, work involvement, and activity preference (a preference by the worker to keep himself active and busy on his job). However, subscales for some extrinsic values, such as, attitude toward earnings, social status of job, upward striving and responsibility to work were also included in SWV.

Wollack *et al.*; conducted a series of studies using their Survey of Work Values and found many significant results. They found variations in SWV scores caused by differences in occupation, sex and some other background variables. Also, white collar workers differed with blue collar workers on different subscales. They used these results to claim validity for the scale. Rigorous statistical examinations established the reliability also. Although, SWV was developed specially for workers, but it was successfully used in the context of adolescents also.

2. As has been indicated in preceding sections, the work values have been classified in numerous ways in the industrial and organizational areas. Among all these classifications, the classification as intrinsic and extrinsic work values has been found more practical, suitable and accommodative of most of classifications. According to this classification, the intrinsic work value involves valuing work for its own sake. It is conceived here as valuing work that is inherently interesting and important and provides autonomy. Work of extrinsic value, however, is valued as a means to attaining instrumental resources separable from the meaning of the work activities themselves, for example, income, security, and prestige. According to Duffy and Sedlacek (2007), intrinsic work values refer to an importance placed on autonomy and interest; whereas extrinsic work values refer to an importance placed on making money and having job security. Here, it should be made clear that intrinsic and extrinsic values are not the opposite poles of a single dimension. Earlier, Wollack, Goodale, Witjing and Smith (1971) had reported findings in support of a dichotomy of two distinct factors; one, work related values (intrinsic values) and the other, reward related values (extrinsic values). The results of later empirical studies have suggested that many people who had higher intrinsic orientations were also the more extrinsically oriented. Mortimer *et al.* (1996) found similar results in their study of adolescent subjects. This point should be seriously noted by teachers and parents.

The classification of work values as intrinsic and extrinsic work values has been widely used in the studies of work values among children also. Lindsay and Knox (1984) analyzed data for 1972 and 1979 from the National Longitudinal Study of the high school seniors (N=9208) and substantiated the findings of Mortimer and Lorence (1979) which had suggested a high degree of temporal stability of intrinsic and extrinsic work values. However, on the basis of their analysis, they further reported that this stability gets moderated by the influences of some factors; such as education, family environment, socio-economic status and socialization. Later, Mortimer and Lorence had divided intrinsic work values into further two categories: (1) the use of abilities, expression of interests, and creativity; and (2) people-oriented concerns, such as the chance to work with people and be useful to society. But they had not used this classification in their study. Lindsay and Knox, in their study, tried to verify this classification also and found it really valid and quite applicable. It highlighted the broader scope of intrinsic motivation.

Johnson (2005) found that those who as adolescents placed greater importance on extrinsic work rewards than did their age-mates continued to place higher importance on these rewards than their age-mates in early adulthood. The same pattern occurred for intrinsic work values also. Whites and those from more highly educated families placed less importance on extrinsic work rewards in early adulthood than the others. The study by Johnson (2005) further indicated that educational attainment fostered intrinsic work values. It was in consistent with prior researches (Lindsay and Knox, 1984). Educational attainment had a negative effect on extrinsic work values. It corroborates that education enhances an emphasis on the intrinsic values of work while it causes less importance to be placed on the extrinsic values of the job. Possibly due to it the young people who obtain higher levels of education become particularly less concerned with job security.

3. An other point, which significantly emerged in the studies on children's work values, is that work values and aspirations take shape during childhood and adolescence. The youths enter the transition to adulthood, according to this view, with well defined work orientations (Johnson, 2001). Despite of this fact, as Mortimer *et al.* (1996) has suggested, the sources of adolescents' work values are not yet well understood. The same has been found about the occupational values also. According to Johnson (2002), although the research on the development of occupational values is limited, researchers suggest that occupational values form during childhood and

adolescence. The findings of his study, in general, indicated that individuals' work values changed substantially during this period of the life course during the process of development with average trajectories of work values indicating some growing realism with age. Research by Lindsay and Knox (1984) has demonstrated that adolescents' values are relatively stable over time. Mortimer *et al.* (1996) reported that adolescents' values are initially variable and become more stable over time. Marini, *et al.* (1996) also examined the changes in work values during adolescence and early childhood. They found decline in at least three domains of work values during this phase of development. The three domains were extrinsic, altruistic and social work values.

The results of the study of Weisgram (2006) indicated that children and young adolescents were idealistic in their endorsement of work values. This was in consistent with the findings of another research by Johnson (2002) on older adolescents. One can guess that this idealism gets transformed with the experiences of realities of life during the development process in later developmental stages. It is the phase during which not only the wok values, but all types of values among adolescents are variable up to certain extent. This point is relevant in the sense that during this phase interventions in order to instil positive work values may be quite effective.

4. The third point is about the role of family, society and socialization in shaping work values among children. Socialization in all societies involves an introduction to the sober world of adult responsibilities. It gives training to children for appropriate adult roles (Kaestle, 1978). Loughlin and Barling (1998) has argued that the work is a major socialization agent in adolescent development.

   Johnson (2002) had concluded on the basis of findings of his study that work values trajectories were systematically tied to social origins and early experiences. Gender played an important role in the changes in work values. The work values of young black women, for example, changed the most as they came to terms with their occupational opportunities. It suggested the roles of race also. However, the rates of change in values was not similar across racial and gender groups. Johnson (2002) was of the view that the transition from adolescence to adulthood constitutes a critical time in formation of life pathways. Therefore, the nature of subsequent changes that may occur in work values during this time along with its links to key aspects of social origins and adolescent experiences in school and work provide a valid area of scientific investigations. Different frameworks have pointed to the roles of factors of social origins, such as social class and gender in children's and adolescents' developing work values (Marini, Pi-Ling, Erica and Ann, 1996; Johnson, 2001).

The studies have also revealed that work values are usually transmitted from parents to child. For example, if father likes working with people or data or things—his son will probably learn the same work values (Mortimer, 1999). This would particularly be the case when there are close and empathetic relationship between parent and child. Duffy and Sedlacek (2007) in his study based on factor analysis method, found that the children of median parental income groups preferred more to intrinsic work values. Another great influence on work values is the person's colleagues. The studies, conducted on students have indicated that: (1) students learn from both faculty and peers, and (2) also, they learn through socialization in both formal and informal (coincidental) manner.

There are a number of studies which have revealed that many of the background variables, such as gender, socio-economic status, race, community and social class—all affect the work values among the adolescents. These effects happen through the process of socialization. The study by Leong and Tata (1990) can be seen as an example of such studies. They expressed the view that since Asians in general, and Chinese in particular, have tended to be more group-oriented and collectivistic people when compared with White Americans, they may differ in their work values orientations. Their view was supported by the results of their study. They had used the Ohio Work Values Inventory (OWVI) in their study of work values among a group of Chinese-American children (5th and 6th graders). The subjects were 177 Chinese-American fifth and sixth graders in a Los Angeles inner-city elementary school composed of mainly Chinese-

American students. The sample consisted of 98 fifth graders (44.9% boys and 55.1% girls) and 79 sixth graders (35.4% boys and 64.6% girls). They had claimed that although the study was based on a sample of convenience, the Chinese-American children of the sample were quite representative of Chinese-American children of inner-city elementary schools. They found differences between work values of high acculturation children and low-acculturation children of this community. On the ground of their findings Leong and Tata (1990) advised counsellors to make more interventions at grade school levels to make children more aware of different options of vocational/work values, while still respecting the cultural values of their community. This advice is more valid in the context of multicultural society of India. Johnson (2002) also had reported that the communities differ in the values they hold and encourage in children. Members of rural communities were found to be often less materialistic and more conservative in orientation. Adolescents from farming families embraced stronger altruistic work values and attached less importance to money and materialism. Wollack *et al.* (1971) had found variations in Survey of Work Values (SWV) scores caused by differences in occupation, sex and some other background variables. The results were consistent with the hypothesized two-factor dichotomy of work related values (intrinsic values) and reward related values (extrinsic values). Also, white-collar workers differed with blue-collar workers on different subscales.

Friedlander (2006) also found variations in work values across white collar and blue collar occupations in his study. It was found that the self-actualization aspects were of prime importance to white-collar workers, and the social environment was of paramount value to blue-collar workers. Only minor variations in work values were found across adjacent status levels, although status and occupational levels interacted with work characteristics and had differential effects on work hierarchies. Earlier Sagy (1997) had obtained in his research differences in work values of students of two different cultures. Apart from them, several other factors, for example, race, the type of community in which they grow up, and connections to religious institutions also are found to determine the development of work values among children of this transitional phase. The results of some earlier studies have already indicated that the work values develop as a function of parents' socio-economic status at initial level also. Johnson (2002) further expressed view that beyond social origins, adolescents enter the transition to adulthood with varying academic and work related experiences. These results seem to be of special significance from the children's development point of view. Thus it can be safely concluded here on the basis of findings of all these studies that the factors, having social origins, determine different domains of work values significantly. However, the intensity of such determining effect varies across different domains of work values.

The association between family and work values has been established by several studies. The family is a primary institution, where children get socialized. It has been concluded on the basis of researches that the relationship between work values and family is bi-directional. Whereas most of the researches concentrate on demonstrating the effects of family on work values, some studies have indicated that work orientations affect family; sometimes shape the prospects of marriage and parenthood. Johnson (2005) found similar results in his study. The study by Johnson (2005) was based on the analyses of data from the Youth Development Study, a longitudinal study that began in 1988 with a randomly chosen panel of 1,000 ninth-grade students enrolled in the St. Paul Public School district in Minnesota. He found that stronger extrinsic work values and weaker intrinsic work values in adolescence were associated with marrying and with having children by age 26-27. He discussed his findings to argue that 'of course, these are issues of timing, as young people with low extrinsic work values and those with high intrinsic work values do not necessarily forgo marriage and parenthood but enter them at older ages on average'. Johnson also found that work values across family statuses also differ with each other. It was a significant indication of the role of status of a person in his family in determining his work values.

5. It has been unequivocally accepted that the educational processes play vital role in developing work values among school children. Despite it, the modern formal education programmes focus almost exclusively on imparting physical, social and mental skills only. They place very little conscious emphasis on the attitudes, the mental understandings and decisiveness, and the psychological values needed for these skills to result in achievement and fulfilment (Patil, 2008). Therefore, the educationists are frequently arguing to use education system in order to generate proper work values among the students. Nnaike, U. (2008) has recently commented that an education system that does not produce relevant people is not worth its name. Therefore, he suggested the teachers to instil values in their students. Neumann and Neumann (1983) were also of the view that the education system can use instilling work values as a mechanism to develop a good work culture in the society.

   The impacts of all the aspects of education system and processes on development adequate values including the work values have been investigated in several studies. The findings of such studies have provided relevant knowledge about work values in the specific context of children. For example, Johnson (2001) studied the work values of students of High School classes and found that almost all of these students rate the jobs at top that are interesting to do.

   Among different educational experiences, school curriculum seems to be one of most potent determinants that could influence patterns of stability and change in work values during the transition. The relationship of schools and school-activities with the work and work values has been established in many studies. For example, Staff and Mortimer (2007), in their study found that moderate work—assigned to children of late adolescent stage coupled with school works appears to especially facilitate the educational attainment of low promise youth.

   Discipline is a inseparable component of all types of school activities. It has been found relevant contributor to work orientation of school going children. According to Kaestle (1978), there is much evidence to support the view that school discipline determine the future work discipline.

Perhaps that was the reason that the parents in nineteenth century America wanted schools to take custody of their children, and wanted schools to train their children in basic skills and attitudes with discipline. Kaestle presented the pattern of historical shift in the purposes, methods, and importance of school discipline from eighteenth century to nineteenth century in America. He opined that in the eighteenth century teachers ruled by virtue of their ascribed position, backed by the threat and frequent exercise of the rod. By 1840, in contrast, the authority of teachers and the advisability of corporal punishment were widely discussed in America. New pedagogical schemes, such as the highly regimented monitorial system and the graded school, emphasized that the structure and procedures of schools would themselves shape appropriate character of children, which consequently would shape children into industrious, frugal, emperate, subordinate, trustworthy, brave, clean, and reverent adults. All these arguments of Kaestle (1978) are quite generalizable in Indian context also.

6. The next point which has been established through a large number of studies—conducted on children's work values, is about the role of gender in determining and shaping work values among children. According to Weisgram (2006), the researches have demonstrated that children often behave in ways consistent with their gender schemas. Specifically, children prefer toys that are labelled for their own gender and even discontinue play with attractive toys when they are labelled for the other sex. Thus, gender schema theory predicts that children should prefer occupations that are labelled for their own gender and lose interest in desirable occupations when they are labelled for the other sex. Wiesgram, Bigler and Liben (2010) noted that the distinction between male and female is perhaps the most visible and dramatic subdivision within our species. Within developmental psychology, empirical and theoretical literatures document sex differences in behavioural realms such as play, cognitive skills, peer relations, and educational pathways From a lifespan developmental perspective, one of the most striking domains of gender differentiation occurs in the world of work. Substantial sex differences in career interests are evident in

preschoolers, elementary school-age children, adolescents, and adults. Wiesgram *et al.* (2010) have conducted exhaustive researches divided into two parts. The results of their study suggested that sex differences in work values were quite cognizable and it seemed to lead to sex-typed occupational interests in adult stage. Furthermore, according to them, this pathway seems to develop gradually, beginning in childhood and strengthening across adolescence. Data from Study indicated that sex differences in occupational values (with males tending to endorse money and power values, and females tending to endorse altruistic and family values) were evident in adults and, to a limited extent, in adolescents, but not in children. On the basis of results of their two studies, Wiesgram *et al.* (2010) concluded that work fulfils personal values, perhaps differently for males and females.

Leong and Tata (1990) used the Ohio Work Values Inventory (OWVI) in their study of work values among a group of children of 5th and 6th graders. They found some sex differences among this group of children: boys valued object orientation, self-realization, and ideas-data more than did girls, and girls valued altruism more than did boys. Abu-Saad and Isralowitz (1997) conducted a study to examine the gender differences in work values. The sample consisted 820 undergraduate students of Israel. Among them 391 were males and 429 were female students. The results suggested gender differences in work values, but only up to a limited extent. In the study of Duffy and Sedlacek (2007) also, there was more liking of extrinsic values among male students, while the female students liked more to social values. Marini, *et al.* (1996) had found that the women assigned more importance to intrinsic and altruistic rewards than men, whereas men assigned more importance to influence and leisure than women. Of course a consistent pattern of such differences have been seen in different studies, conducted in this area. It corroborated the significance of impact of gender on work values. It was by no way unexpected. The gender has been found to determine almost all types of psychological and developmental attributes. (In a recent interesting study of St. Claire, Hayward and Rogers (2010), it was found that Coffee helps women to cope with stressful meetings but has the opposite effect on men).

7. The studies have suggested a clear link between the work values of children and relative liking for different careers for future life. One of such studies was conducted by Duffy and Sedlacek (2007) who examined the significance of different factors of work values in career choice. They surveyed 3570 first year college students regarding the factors they deemed most important to their long-term career choice. The results of this survey suggested that the factors of work values predict career choice significantly, therefore, the career counsellors should be encouraged to place a great emphasis on the role of work values. The data indicate that a focus on work values in career counselling may be useful for incoming first year college students. Earlier Luzzo (2000) also had viewed work values to be critical in career counselling processes. There is nearly a consensus that an individual's career choice is strongly influenced by the work values that he or she holds (Liu and Lei, 2012).

Neumann and Neumann (1983) adopted definition of work values proposed by Super and examined the power of Super's work values in discriminating between engineering and liberal Arts students. Super had defined work values as the qualities people desire and seek in the activities in which they engage and in the situations where they live. On the basis of his definition, Super had developed three dimensions of work values. Neumann and Neumann conducted three analyses, one for each of these different dimensions. The major findings suggested that all three dimensions discriminate effectively between the two categories of students, the work values which discriminate in favour of liberal arts students tend to focus on general aspects of the work, and the work values favouring engineering students are values relevant to specific aspects of their perceived jobs.

Another aspect of relationship between work values and professional career was exposed in a study conducted by Salemela-Aro, Tolvanen and Numi (2009). They found poor work ethic at university level education predicting burnout seventeen years later. In their study Salmela-Aro and colleagues recruited 292 students and had them complete the "success expectation scale" and the "task-avoidance scale" and then followed them many years later and asked them to fill in measures of work burnout and work engagement. Turning the results the other way around, students who were optimistic and focused at university tended to be more engaged in their working lives and to avoid burnout. The researchers said that so-called "achievement strategies" are more modifiable than personality traits and that there could, therefore, be value in university interventions that promote optimistic strategies and reduction in task avoidance.

Interestingly, Miceli and Castelfranchi (2002) also have highlighted that optimism and pessimism determine the work orientation of an individual. Optimism is generally seen as a good strategy in that people's positive beliefs about their future outcomes favour continued striving and eventually actual success; while pessimistic attitudes work as self-fulfilling prophecies by favouring disengagement from future efforts and leading to actual failure. Also, pessimists are less likely than optimists to employ adaptive coping strategies in stressful tasks (Kaiser, Major and McCoy, 2004). Contradicting it some other studies have interestingly shown that in some situations, pessimism helps us see things more accurately. It actually sharpens our sense of troubling realities in work situations. (Retrieved from *www.rediff.com/money/2007/au/28book.htm*).

On the basis of review, it can be concluded that the factors, such as gender, characteristics of communities, race, family characteristics and socio-economic status determine the work values among children also. The empirical researches have substantiated it up to a significant extent (e.g., Abu-Saad and Isralowitz, 1997; Perrone, Selacek and Alexander, 2001; Duffy and Sedlacek, 2007). Also, different components of educational programmes shape the work values of children. Therefore, the educational programmes can be used for the purpose of instilling adequate work values among students. Later, these students would be human capital of great qualities for the society or nation.

Silvino (1996) has noted that the fact that the value formations have early beginnings and one's behaviour is influenced by the values he holds, gives strong support for the need to study values at the elementary school level. With this assumption he himself planned a study and examined the values of 555 of grade four, five and six to determine if significant value differences exist across sex, grade, socio-economic status and types of school. The results were in favour of significant value differences. While analyzing the results of his study, Silvino suggested that if value differences exist among elementary school children, then attention should be given to possible value conflicts within schools or classrooms which might lead to some negative incidents. For this purpose, he advised to develop a teachers training programme in order to provide prospective teachers with abilities to deal more creatively with individual differences in the classroom. This section of review is closed here with an acceptance of the conclusive arguments of Silvino to use it as the rationales for the planning of a study.

2

Planning, Procedure and Findings of the Study

Planning of a Study

The theoretical elaborations that provided rationales in different ways to the planning of a new study—discussed in this dissertation, are reported first in this chapter. To begin, let us quote Rodgers (1980) as saying: '*Nothing is more certain or important about childhood than the leaving of it. Ultimately, the protective layers of dependency essential to infancy must be stripped away, swaddling cloths exchange for new roles and costumes a children propelled into adulthood. Above all, the propensity to play must somehow be supplanted by a willingness to assume those burdens—which by common consent form a society's work' (p. 354)*. It clearly suggests that the transformation of a 'nonworking baby' as a 'working member of society' is certain and essential. The dynamics of such transformation is always relevant area of scientific investigations. Rodgers (1980) further opined that along with the fictions written for the children and child rearing advices offered to parents and practiced by them, the routine of schools is an important factor that determines the above said transformation. In fact, the work values germinate either in family or in classrooms. Since the work values are regarded to be most central and conspicuous values of the modern years, therefore, it seems necessary to intervene in classroom systems in order to develop adequate work values among today's children—who would have to own responsibilities of nation tomorrow. S. Shukla (2004) contended that here is a high mounting demand for an ideal educational system based on the philosophy of optimum development of three basic faculties—heart, head and hand (*Vidya, Vivek* and *Kaushal*). Certainly the faculty of *Kaushal* is manifestation of appropriate work values.

Most contemporary observers believe that today's children do not work. One can ask—Why? To respond this question, we have to examine the efficacy of our various systems, including the educational system, in creating work values among our children. What Strauss (1962) has emphasized in early sixties of last century is equally relevant today also. He was of the view that new researches are always needed on the implications of children's chores for their personal development as well as for development of society. Through these chores, the children learn the values, identify with the parental motivations and make them prepare for adult roles. The present project was developed in the context of the assumptions similar to stated above.

The focus of present study was on the work values in the specific context of children. The area of work values in children seems to be very relevant area for scientific interests because most of the studies have indicated that work values and aspirations take shape during childhood and adolescence. The youths enter the transition to adulthood, according to this view, with well defined work orientations (Johnson, 2001). Loughlin and Barling (1998) also expressed the view that the students typically form their work values, identity, and career aspirations during teen age years. Despite of this fact, as Mortimer (1996) has suggested, the sources of adolescents' work values are not yet well understood.

The reports from Kothari Commission to Ram Murti Committee, all have reiterated the value of work as an essential part of educational processes. The National Policy of Education (1986) and the current National Framework on Education have given emphasis on promoting work values in students. National leaders like Mahatma Gandhi, Lokmanya Tilak and Vinoba Bhave also gave tremendous emphasis on work values in the process of education. At present some provisions for work has been made in the schooling system through physical education, work experience and vocational learning. All this has not been very much helpful in developing and shaping work values and work ethic. It is evident from the way dishonesty, bribery and various malpractices are becoming part and parcel of work life. Also, the significance of punctuality, commitment, responsibility, cooperation at work place and pride in effort is losing its earlier grace and charm in the mind of the masses. Increasingly larger number of public sector enterprises is becoming sick and are being privatized because of lack of profit, low productivity and low organizational effectiveness. They are facing difficulty in sustaining growth and development.

While such a situation is caused by many factors, the decline in respect for and practice of work values is one major cause. In modern India, independence opened a new era of hopes, ambitions and desires. A section of Indian urban people, trained in Western education, became individualistic. The caste-profession linkage got weakened, social and geographical mobility increased, and the social structure changed to a large extent during last few decades in the country. The family system moved from joint to nuclear pattern. The vocationalization and professionalization of jobs further contributed a non-social and mechanized work orientation. The achievement orientation along with individualism motivated people to work for the enhancement of personal accomplishments without having concerns for group or community. It led to develop an orientation that made them more concerned with the individual benefits.

It is apparent that most of the work values, which have gained currency in our country after Independence, are achievement-oriented and are based on maximizing gains by incurring minimum efforts. It is a general thinking now that the personal gains should be more and more even at the cost of society. It is unfortunate that after a half century of gaining political independence the society, in general, has not been able to establish and promote work values among its citizens. Today, attainment of 'money' by any means has assumed high priority. The consumerist and materialist pursuits in life have left everything behind. It is a matter of grave concern that instead of hard work people go for short cuts and people from almost all walks of life (e.g., business, politics, bureaucracy, and academia) are found to engage in malpractices of various kinds to acquire assets through wrong means. It is a painful fact that all types of morality and virtue, which should have been integral part of work, have moved to background due to these short cuts and malpractices. One can remember that morality is generally defined as a set of rules that enables people to live and work together in harmony and virtue involves internalizing those rules (Baumeister and Exline, 1999). Thus, the work values should develop among us as virtues then only we would be able to work for personal as well as community level gains.

Work values are usually transmitted from parents to child. For example, if father likes working with people or data or things—his son will probably learn the same work values (Mortimer, 1999). This would particularly be the case when there are close and empathetic relationship between parent and child. Another great influence on work values is the person's colleagues. The studies, conducted on students have indicated that: (1) students learn from both faculty and peers, and (2) also, they learn through socialization in both formal and informal (coincidental) manner. The educational processes play vital role in developing work values among school children.

The above analysis suggested at least two points. First, work values are acquired either through socialization or through learning in educational institutions. Second, work values determine the psychological feedback of the work being done, in the from of pleasure or anxiety or stress. On the basis of these points also, it seems relevant to conceptualize and operationalize the work values among school going children.

In the contemporary period we find ourselves placed in a peculiar situation in which there is contrast between a strong cultural context of values and ethics, and practice of values as evidenced in the contemporary social life. This leads to ambiguity in the views of young minds that are growing and shall be part of future citizenship of the society. If left unchecked, this situation may create problems in the progress of country. Some of the studies have indicated about some indigenous factors, which have adversely affected the value development in our country. Tiwari (2003), in an empirical study, noted that a belief that "own behaviour cannot determine the occurrence of the outcomes or reinforcements they seek" had overinfluenced the thinking of most of us. We believe that the 'action-consequence' association has been badly damaged in our system and has become quite unpredictable due to interferences of vested interests. Therefore, we feel less motivated to work. Certainly such a situation might bar the development of proper work values among people of country. In the nation, which is passing through a transitional phase of development, this points need to be addressed from every corner.

It is very genuine to expect from the educational sector to take lead in dealing with these issues, relevant to development of positive work values among students. The educational sector has the real formal responsibility of building a better block of future society. With this in view, the present study proposes to map the context of work values and assessing the values held by school children.

The nation has made commitment to move forward and a vision for 2020 has been advanced in which India is projected to be a super power and a self-reliant country. This vision can be realized only when society engages in sincere effort, means business and commits to positive work values. Unfortunately, not only our students, most of people of our country do not show adequate work values. They have a tendency to avoid 'work' and have interests in shortcuts or foul measures to achieve their goals. It is causing a variety of imbalances in society, therefore, it is being seriously felt that this issue should be addressed at every possible level. Here the educationists and social scientists of related fields have a major role to play. They will have to explore the means and modalities to develop and nurture work values. For this purpose, schools appear as one of the most important sites for relevant intervention. Silvino (1996), an American psychologist commented that our nation's schools and the education that our children are receiving have been subjected to much criticism in recent years. However, one of the strongest criticisms of our school's inability to incorporate humanistic aspects of education into its curriculum has been voiced by several scholars working in related areas. This inability of the schools have left "children to encounter the complexities of values with no strategy to guide them" (Huyssen, 1970, p. 27—quoted by Silvino, 1996). These critical comments of Silvino on American schooling is safely generalizable in total in the context of Indian schooling.

The present research proposal is based on the assumptions and arguments—discussed above. It intends to explore the possibilities of interventions in the schooling system for a healthy reform in it. It can be regarded to be a beginning in the direction of bringing work values in the centre of school education.

Operationalization of Work Value in the Specific Context of School Going Children

As has been frequently reported the work values have been extensively researched in the industrial and organizational fields. However, only a few investigations of work values in the specific context of children are available in literature. They have not been able to suggest the well agreed operationalization of the work value among children. It means that the area is still of vague nature. Therefore, any attempt to operationalize the work value in the school going children would always be open for clarification seeking questions. The same happened with the present project. Initially when the proposal was placed before the committee of experts associated with ERIC, NCERT for consideration, the committee wanted clarification about the way of operationalization of work value—particularly in the context of elementary education. The Principal Investigator produced modified proposal, which contained the desired clarification. It was stated in the revised proposal that the work values of the students of elementary level might be certainly operationalized in terms of attributes such as:

1. Likelihood to accept and owning the works/assignments,
2. Perception of desirability of work,
3. Love for the works and enjoyment in doing it,
4. Ability to distinguish between work and non-work,
5. Sharing the feelings of parents about work, and
6. Evaluation of instrumentality of works to achieve the desired objectives.

Later the proposal was approved by the committee of experts. Along with the clarification, the proposal presented assumption that two considerations seem to offer rationales for operationalizing work values among children. They are as given below:

(A) Children perceive that their parents and other adults around them are continuously engaged in one or other type of work. They feel that the work is instrumental to achieve the precious things. Even the bread and butter of the family are based on the works. They and their family are identified on the basis of the works done by the family members. Therefore, they learn to recognize the significance of the works. Also, they try to share the feelings about the works with the other members of their families.

(B) The school going children are given home works/assignments. They experience a link between completion of the assignments and physical or psychological reward.

It should be further made clear that the operationalization of work value in the present study was done in the manner that suited with the objectives of the study. The general objective of the study was to explore and identify the work values among Junior High School students.

Major Objectives of the Study

The major objective of the proposal was to target the content of 'work values' in school education. In particular, it would attend to the following objectives:

1. Identification of the work values available in curriculum—presently being taught at Jr. High School level.
2. Study the pattern of preferences and practices of work values prevailing among the students.
3. Developing a work value scale—valid for students of Jr. High School level.
4. Examining the variations in work values in relation to contextual variables (see Tan and Khoo, 2002). To this end gender, ecological, and family related variations in work values and its developmental trend would be analyzed.
5. Examining the views of the stakeholders (e.g., parents, teachers, school administrators) in regard to work values.

Specific Research Questions (Problems)

In view of the preceding considerations it seems relevant to identify work values and its development in children. The basic premise is that the education may play an important role in this sphere. Therefore, it seems appropriate to target students for this purpose. The present research plan proposes to deal with the following specific problems:

1. What is the status of work values in the curriculum of grades 6 to 8?
2. How do the parents, teachers and school administrators think about work values?
3. How do the school children define work? What are their attitudes towards works?

4. How can a reliable scale of work value—valid for students of Jr. High School level, be developed?
5. How do the various aspects of socio-cultural context relate to work values and work attitudes?

Procedure, Methodology and Findings

The study was conducted in three phases (Phases 1 to 3). Each of these phases had different objectives that needed to adopt different methodology. The objective and the methodology—adopted in every phase of the study and its outcomes/findings are reported separately.

Phase 1: Counting of 'Work' Related Themes in Text-Books prescribed for Classes of Jr. High School Level

The first research question was addressed in this phase. The question was: 'What is the status of work values in the curriculum of grades 6 to 8?' In an attempt to answer this question, all the text-books of Hindi, English and Social Studies of grades 6th to 8th prescribed by CBSE and U.P. Board, Allahabad were content analyzed to find out the themes related to 'work' in this phase. These themes were counted. Initially we felt that such contents are very rarely available in these text-books. The teachers of these classes suggested that at these levels the emphases are on to provide basic knowledge, to develop study habits and interests. None (not even the guardians) is concerned about the work values among these students. It is evident from the tendency of most of the guardians to complete the home works of their children themselves. Some of them employ tutors for this purpose.

However, we thoroughly scanned the text-books and noted all the direct or indirect references of work related concepts. Despite all our efforts and leniencies, we could find only 39 themes in total, which were referred at one or more than one places in some forms in these text-books. The total number of references were 83, only. Certainly it is very less in number. These references, too, were available in very superficial manner and seemed to be unable to have any significant impact at most of the time. In our view it needs special attention.

The detailed listing of these themes along with the number of places (frequency) of their references in the text-books of Jr. High School level books, are presented in following Box. (Box 2.1). As is evident from the box, only a few work related themes have appeared at more than one place in the text-books. For example, importance of cooperation with other in works was found at six places. Similarly, work for society and nation, and inspirations to work from parents or other family members—who are always seen working had appeared at five places. Pleasure and satisfaction after work completion and professional works and scope of enhancement of its opportunities—both were available in text-books four times. Some other important work related themes; such as, variety and importance of works for meals (bread and butter), work in childhood or children's works, hard work in study, commitments toward works, and usefulness of machines in works were found at three different places in these text-books.

It was disappointing that some very essential and important attributes of work or work value got miserably under-represented in the text-books. For example, all of us admire Gandhi as a hard worker and perceive him as the role model for doing one's work by oneself, but this aspect of Gandhi is referred only twice in these text-books. Similarly, the association between hard work and success, or relationship between work and self-esteem, or relation between *Aaram* and *Kaam* were available twice, only. Furthermore, some other such themes, which seemed to be very pertinent from the work-value point of view, were available only once in these books. Some examples of such themes are; lessons to work hard from animals, women's literacy and its positive impacts on their works, work on time or punctuality in work, work while you work, play while you play, and do not avoid working due to risk factors.

Box 2.1: The 'work' related themes and their frequency of availability in text-books of Jr. High School classes

S. No.	*'Work' related Themes*	*Frequency of Availability*
1.	Importance of cooperation with each other in works	6
2.	Work for society and nation	5
3.	Inspirations to work from parents or other family members, who are always seen working	5
4.	Pleasure and satisfaction after work completion	4
5.	Professional works and scope of enhancement of its opportunities	4
6.	Works by British rulers including the acts of 'divide and rule'.	4

(Contd.)

Box 2.1 (*Contd.*)

S. No.	*'Work' related Themes*	*Frequency of Availability*
7.	Variety and importance of works for meals (bread and butter)	3
8.	Work in childhood or Children's works	3
9.	Hard work in study	3
10.	Commitments towards works	3
11.	Usefulness of machines in works	3
12.	Obstacles in works	3
13.	Importance of agricultural works	2
14.	Gandhi as the role model for doing one's work by oneself	2
15.	Administrative works	2
16.	Non-rewarding works	2
17.	Social works	2
18.	Benefits of being careful while working	2
19.	Works of plantation	2
20.	Association between hard work and success	2
21.	Work and self-esteem	2
22.	Relation between *Aaram* and *Kaam*	2
23.	Expansion of scope of works from agriculture to offices and industries	1
24.	Works to transform some raw products into some valuable and useful goods	1
25.	Work as the hobby	1
26.	Works of servants	1
27.	Industrial works	1
28.	Lessons to work hard from animals	1
29.	Women's literacy and its positive impacts on their works	1
30.	Work on time or Punctuality in work	1
31.	Work while you work, play while you play	1
32.	Do not avoid working due to risk factors	1
33.	Abilities matter in the works, not the heavy shape or size	1
34.	Laws associated with works are helpful	1
35.	To overcome physiological disabilities to do one's works	1
36.	Problems of dishonesty and dutilessness in government offices	1
37.	Learning through works	1
38.	To work even in the state of acute sadness	1
39.	Works as the measure to express one's love or other feelings toward others	1
	Total	**83**

Phase 2: Current Work Values among Children—How Do the Different Stakeholders Perceive?

One major objective of the project was to examine the views of different stakeholders about the existing work values among children. Therefore, in this phase of project, 30 students, 20 teachers, 30 parents and 20 administrative staff (serving in educational set-up) were interviewed to collect relevant information with the help of a semi structured interview schedule, which consisted questions about the meaning of work, attitude towards work and work values. This interview schedule was developed on the basis of informal consultations with 10 teachers having at least ten years experience of teaching at Jr. High School alongwith 5 guardians, who were professors of B. Ed. faculty. This faculty prepares the teachers for teaching at Jr. High School level. During the consultations, they were first told the objectives and mode of investigations of the project. On the basis of these consultations a large number of questions were developed. They were sorted and edited yielding 54 questions for final considerations. Then after a formal meeting with them was organized to examine the practical relevance of these questions in the context of the purpose and objectives of the task. However, in this meeting only 8 teachers and 4 guardians could participate. In this meeting each of the 54 questions were considered, separately and a schedule containing 22 questions was finally developed. This schedule was used in the interview.

The information obtained from the interviews of above stated 100 respondents were appropriately analyzed and percentages of respondents giving each possible answer of a question were calculated. Some very interesting results were found. While doing so, it was noted that the opinions—expressed by students, teachers, parents and administrative staff did not differ with each other noticeably, so it was decided to combine their answers to the questions given by them. These questions, along with the answers, and the percentage of respondents giving a particular answer, are presented in Box 2.2.

In general, the parents, teachers and administrative staffs showed full faith in the potential of children to learn work values. For example, 73 per cent of respondents were of the view that the students of classes 6th to 8th understand the meaning of work. If a student does not understand it, it is due to the slackness of guardians, teachers and society. Further obtained answers revealed that in stakeholders' opinions, the children not only understand the meaning of 'work', they know the benefits of work, they get inspirations from the parents and elders of the family to work hard, they are capable to enjoy the pleasure of completing the tasks, and also are aware about the role of work for the livelihood of family. However, the stakeholders have also opined that the children studying at Jr. High School level do not like work. They take it as the burden. These children have clear negative feelings, particularly towards physical-labour based work. It was interesting to note that according to the stakeholders, the present education system was more to blame for poor work values among children. It provides logical support to the presumption of present study, according to which the interventions are needed in present education system in order to develop proper work values in students.

Box 2.2 : Questions asked to the Respondents, answers given by them and Percentage of Respondents giving the particular answer

S. No. of Que.	*Questions and Obtained Answers from the Respondents*	*Percentage of Respondents*
1.	Do the students of Jr. High School understand the meaning of work?	
	• Yes	73
	• No	23
2.	How do they mean work?	
	• Homework	64
	• To do—as asked by elders	52
	• To accomplish the responsibility	47
	• To shape future	38
	• Sports/Games	38
	• Domestic works	22
3.	If they do not understand the meaning of work, what are the reasons?	
	• Slackness of guardians	58
	• Slackness of teachers	35
	• Slackness of society	31
4.	Should these students understand the meaning of work? If yes, in what form?	
	• As the means to achieve goals or success	52
	• As the labour	51
	• As the achieving education	49
	• As the skill enhancement	20

(*Contd.*)

Box 2.2 (*Contd.*)

S. No. of Que.	*Questions and Obtained Answers from the Respondents*	*Percentage of Respondents*
5.	Rank the works in accordance to the liking of children	
	• To play	100
	• Bicycling	48
	• Study	35
	• Domestic works	20
	• Mathematical or scientific works	18
6.	What type of works should be assigned to the students of Jr. High School level?	
	• The work of their interest	64
	• The work that helps in their physical and mental development	57
	• Domestic work	49
	• Reading books	49
	• Homework	43
	• The works of physical labour and exercises	40
7.	How do they view works?	
	• As the burden	81
	• Beneficial	43
	• As a responsibility	21
	• Helplessness	19
8.	How far do these students seriously understand the importance of work for livelihood of family?	
	• Very much	58
	• A little	10
	• Not at all	22
	• Deprived children understand up to great extent	80
9.	What type of work would they prefer in their future?	
	• The work giving more money	78
	• The work giving name and fame	74
	• The hereditary work	61
	• Easy or Comfortable	33
	• Work of army	21
10.	Do the students of such family, where all the members are employed, get more inspired for hard work?	
	• Yes	63
	• No	23
11.	Do these students understand the benefits of works involving physical labour?	
	• Yes	47
	• No	53

(*Contd.*)

Box 2.2 (*Contd.*)

S. No. of Que.	Questions and Obtained Answers from the Respondents	Percentage of Respondents
12.	What type of benefits?	
	• Health	77
	• Agility or Smartness	54
	• Making money	33
	• Physical strength	31
13.	What does the education, offered at Jr. High School, tell the students regarding the importance of work?	
	• To do hard work	48
	• For betterment of future	36
	• Means of progress	32
	• Gives praises	27
14.	What is the method—useful to tell importance of work?	
	• Practical	41
	• Theoretical	07
	• Both	52
15.	What are the reasons for completing home assignments wholeheartedly?	
	• Cooperation and encouragement from the family	79
	• Desire to be praised in class	46
	• Personal interest or dedication	42
16.	What are the reasons for not taking interest in completing home assignment?	
	• To take it as the burden	59
	• Family environment	35
	• Bad company	30
	• TV	27
17.	How to convince the non-working children to work?	
	• Through love and affection	82
	• Warning to complain at the home	67
	• Warning to be fail in the examination	51
	• Comparing with other students of class	31
	• Scolding	31
	• Physical punishment	15
18.	Their opinions about homework?	
	• The burden	67
	• Routine work of daily	58
	• Responsibility of family	37
	• A method of study	17
19.	If the children do not understand the importance of work, who is responsible?	

(*Contd.*)

Box 2.2 (*Contd.*)

S. No. of Que.	*Questions and Obtained Answers from the Respondents*	*Percentage of Respondents*
	• Present education system	63
	• Teachers	36
	• Parents	29
	• Children themselves	9
	• All of them	7
20.	Name some works that help in physical and mental development.	
	• Sports competition	53
	• Computer based work	47
	• Essay competition	23
	• Debates	21
	• Yogic exercises	16
21.	Can the students feel pleasure on completion of work?	
	• Yes	82
	• No	18
22.	Do the students of Jr. High School classes know the benefits of doing work?	
	• Yes	66
	• No	18

Note: The original questions-administered were in Hindi. These items are presented in Appendix 'A'. Here, the English translation of the items are presented just for convenience of presentation and understanding.)

Phase 3: Development of a Scale of Work Value of Children and Examination of Variations in Work Values Across Some Factors

This phase was the major part of the study. It can be divided in two parts. The first part (A) was aimed to develop a work value scale valid in the context of children. In the second part (B) this new scale was used to test the work values of children of Jr. High School level, and to examine the differences among the groups of children differing on gender, rural-urban habitation and their classes (6th, 7th and 8th). The two parts of this phase is described below.

(A) Development of Scale of Work Value for Children—Studying at Jr. High School Level

As has been said earlier, the area of work value has been extensively studied in the industrial and organizational fields. In these fields, several scale of work values are developed. However, only a few scales to assess the work values of children are available in literature. The particulars about some of these scales are presented in Section 1. Some scales to measure work values of school going children have been developed in India also. For example, Vasantha (1971) had developed a work value inventory for high school students. Another work value inventory has been developed for adolescents by Dhar (1985). One major objective of the present study was to develop a new reliable and valid scale to measure work values of students at elementary level (particularly for students of Junior High School level). This was done through following steps.

1. First of all, 60 items/statements were written with the help of information collected in Phase 2. With the objective of indigenization, some items were developed on the basis of *Nishkam Karma Yoga*—as is preached in *Srimad Bhagawad Gita*, and were included in the list of items. As has been earlier stated, the *Nishkam Karma Yoga* approach to 'work' is unique contribution of Indian Religious-philosophical tradition. The sixty items, in total, were given to seven departmental colleagues (Department of Psychology, K.S. Saket P.G. College, Ayodhaya) to examine the relevance of each item in measuring work values. They were also requested to judge the communicability of items, specifically in the context of Jr. High School students. The views and responses of these colleagues were utilized to delete some items which, according to them, were not useful for the purpose. Their comments helped in editing some items also. After this exercise, 42 items were included in the first draft of the scale.
2. The 42 items draft was given the shape of a questionnaire and administered to a sample of 240 respondents—selected from different categories as per proposed design. The sample was classified as per the following framework (See Box 2.3).
3. The data obtained from the sample were analyzed using various appropriate statistical methods. Among them the factor analysis method (Principal component analysis) was used with the purpose of developing a work value scale. During the factor analysis, data were rotated that yielded 4 highly significant factors. Each of the four factors had Eigaen

Box 2.3 : Framework of Sample Classification

Gender	*Area*	*Classes*			*Total*
		6	7	8	
Male	Rural	20	20	20	60
	Urban	20	20	20	60
Female	Rural	20	20	20	60
	Urban	20	20	20	60
	Total	**80**	**80**	**80**	**240**

value greater than 2.00 and contributed to not less than 10 per cent of total variation. Later, on the basis of content of items appearing in these factors, the factors were named as; Domestic Work Value (8 items), Knowledge through Work (7 items), Positive Feeling with Works (6 items), and Home Assignment Value (6 items). All the factors were positively operationalized. The factors do not seem consistent with the hypothesized two-factor dichotomy of work values, i.e., intrinsic and extrinsic values.

4. While finalizing the items for these factors, it was noted that some items appeared with equal loadings in more than one factor. Such items were dropped. Since, it was statistically required, therefore, only those items were selected for the factors, which had loading of more than 0.30 in the factor. The factors alongwith the items and their loadings are presented in Boxes 2.4 to 2.7.
5. In the next step, the correlations among all the four factors were computed. The correlations are reported in Table 2.1. As the Table 2.1 shows, all the correlation coefficients were positive and highly significant. The correlation coefficients ranged from 0.18 to 0.50. All of them were significant at.01 level. Therefore, it was decided to develop a single index also for work values by summing scores of all the four factors. Thus a final scale of work value containing sub-scales to assess four factors separately was developed. The coefficient alpha for the final-scale was found to be .76 in the present study. For the sub-scales, it ranged between .67 to .81. (Since one item had appeared in two factors, therefore, the total number of items in final scale were 26). These coefficient

alphas were sufficient to establish the homogeneity of new work value scale and also its sub-scales.

Box 2.4: 1st Factor Work Value: Domestic Work Value

Serial No. of Items	*Items**	*Loading*
1.	How do you feel when your parents or some other elder of the family ask you to do a work?	0.52
4.	Whose responsibility is to accomplish the important domestic works in the family?	0.46
5.	To what extent do you show your eagerness to offer your services to your friends or neighbours in the ceremonies like marriages, etc.?	0.37
7.	To what extent do you attempt wholeheartedly to complete the tasks—assigned to you in the family?	0.44
10.	One should complete the task—assigned to him, treating it as his duty. To what extent do you agree?	0.38
11.	A person has to work to make his future better. Is it true?	0.39
13.	What would happen if none of your family members works?	0.40
23.	How do you feel in serving elderly people of your family, like grand parents?	0.62

* The original items—administered, were in Hindi. These items are presented in Appendix 'B'. Here, the English translation of the items are presented just for convenience of presentation and understanding.)

Box 2.5: 2nd Factor Work Value: Knowledge through Work

Serial No. of Items	*Items**	*Loadings*
6.	How far do you believe that one gets success only up to the extent of his hard work?	0.40
14.	If someone wants his future to be better, he would have to work hard. Is it true?	0.35
16.	Tell your liking for works like study	0.34
17.	Tell your liking for the works that enhance knowledge	0.38
19.	The completion of homework or some other work enhances knowledge and leads to development. Is it true?	0.61
24.	Are you inspired to work hard on seeing people succeed by hard work?	0.34
25.	Should a person still work, even if he is very rich?	0.37

* The original items—administered, were in Hindi. These items are presented in Appendix 'B'. Here the English translation of the items are presented just for convenience of presentation and understanding.

Box 2.6: 3rd Factor Work Value: Positive Feelings with Works

Serial No. of Items	*Items**	*Loadings*
1.	How do you feel when your parents or some other elder of the family ask you to do a work?	0.34
8.	How soon do you get bored with your work?	0.39
9.	How much do you enjoy doing the work that has great significance?	0.36
12.	How do you feel after completing the work—assigned to you?	0.39
15.	Tell your liking for domestic works, such as cleaning of house, doing errands, etc.	0.41
26.	How bad do you feel when you fail in your work?	0.51

* The original items—administered, were in Hindi. These items are presented in Appendix 'B'. Here, the English translation of the items are presented just for convenience of presentation and understanding.

Box 2.7: 4th Factor Work Value: Home Assignment Value

Serial No. of Items	*Items**	*Loadings*
2.	How many students take the home work as a burden?	0.41
3.	What is the role of home work for a student?	0.36
18.	How much do you complete your home work or any other work—assigned to you?	0.54
20.	Do you complete your home work yourself or get it completed by parents or some other elder of the family?	0.35
21.	Do you feel that due to your home work, you do not get time to play?	0.37
22.	Do you pretend doing home work just to avoid domestic or family related works?	0.44

* The original items—administered, were in Hindi. These items are presented in Appendix 'B'. Here the English translation of the items are presented just for convenience of presentation and understanding.

6. Apart from test of homogeneity, attempts were made to further examine the reliability of the finalized scale. For this purpose, the scale was administered on 24 respondents of

Table 2.1: Inter-Correlation Coefficients among Factors of Work Values

Variables	*Domestic Work Value*	*Knowledge through Work*	*Positive Feelings with Works*	*Home Assignment Value*
Domestic Work Value	1.00	—	—	—
Knowledge through Work	0.31**	1.00	—	—
Positive Feelings with Works	0.50**	0.18**	1.00	—
Home Assignment Value	0.42**	0.18**	0.27**	1.00

Note: ** $p < .01$

the sample second time after a time interval of about one month. The correlation between the scores on 26 items—obtained at two times was found to be. 83. It was supportive of reliability of the scale.

7. As for the validity was concerned, at initial level it was claimed that since the scale was developed through the strict standardized procedure with the active help of senior experts of the field, so it had certain face validity. For the further validity check the correlation between total scores on 42 and 26 items was computed. It was found to be 0.74. It can be granted as an strong indicator of validity of scale. Later on some of the findings of present project were also utilized to claim validity.
(The final scale is also enclosed in the Appendix section).

(B) Variations in Work Values in relation to Gender, Rural-Urban Habitation and Schooling Grades

Another objective of the study was to examine the variation in work values due to some contextual variables. So the role of gender, rural-urban habitation and grades of the students (class 6th, 7th and 8th) in such variations was examined.

To investigate the role of gender on work values, first of all the means and standard deviations of the scores of male and female students on factors of work value and also on total work value, were computed. Thereafter, the significance of mean differences based on gender were tested by calculating corresponding t-values. The means, standard deviations and t-values, thus obtained, are reported in Table 2.2.

The comparison between male and female students on different dimensions of work values revealed that the two categories of students did not differ significantly on 'domestic work value' (t value = 0.74). But they differed significantly on the two factors of work value. These factors were; 'knowledge through work' (t=3.36, p < .01) and 'positive feelings with works' (t=2.69, p < .01). It suggested that in comparison to the male students, the female students value more to knowledge through work; and also have more positive feelings with works. The two groups did not differ significantly on home assignment value also (t=0.68). It, interestingly, meant that the boys and girls—both perceive home assignments from the school in similar way. On the total work value scores, the male and female students differed significantly (t=2.54, p < .01). The mean score of female students on 'total work value' was higher in comparison to that of male students that gave the indication of the greater total work value among female students.

Table 2.2: Comparison between Male (N=120) and Female (N=120) Students on Work Values

Variables	*Male Students Mean (SD)*	*Female Students Mean (SD)*	*t-value*
Domestic Work Value	21.95 (2.12)	22.15 (2.02)	0.74
Knowledge through Work	19.82 (1.84)	20.47 (1.06)	3.36**
Positive Feelings with Works	14.40 (1.75)	15.05 (1.99)	2.69**
Home Assignment Value	15.18 (1.93)	15.35 (1.85)	0.68
Total Work Value	68.75 (4.93)	70.30 (4.50)	2.54**

Note: ** p < .01

Table 2.3 presents the mean, standard deviations and the t-values obtained for rural and urban students on variables of work value. There was no significant difference between the mean scores of rural and urban students, except in the case of 'positive feelings with works'. On this factor of work value, the obtained t-value was 3.70 (p < .01). It suggested that the rural students had greater positive feelings with works in comparison to the group of urban students. The absence of significant mean differences on other factors of work value and also on total work value can be regarded to be in partial contrast to the findings of earlier studies, which have shown the significant role of factors of social origins (e.g. Marini, Pi-Ling, Erica and Ann, 1996; Johnson, 2001) in the variations in work value. Thus it seems that the findings of those studies cannot be unquestionably generalized, particularly for the community of students. It would certainly need necessary precautions.

One objective of the study was to examine the variations in work values across schooling grades at Jr. High School level. For this purpose, the means and standard deviations of the scores—obtained by the students of class 6th, 7th and 8th on work value variables were computed, and the significance of differences among these means were tested using one-way analysis of variance method. The means, SDs and corresponding F-values are reported in Table 2.4.

Table 2.3: Comparison between rural (N=120) and urban (N=120) students on work values

Variables	*Rural Mean (SD)*	*Urban Mean (SD)*	*t-value*
Domestic Work Value	22.17 (1.93)	21.93 (2.20)	0.87
Knowledge through Work	19.98 (1.73)	20.30 (1.29)	1.61
Positive Feelings with Works	15.17 (1.70)	14.28 (1.98)	3.70**
Home Assignment Value	15.33 (1.99)	15.20 (1.80)	0.54
Total Work Value	**69.92 (4.51)**	**69.13 (5.01)**	**1.27**

Note: ** p <. 01

The Table 2.4 indicates that the students of class 6th, 7th and 8th differed significantly only on 'home assignment value'. In this case the obtained F-value was 5.87. It was significant at. 01 level. The comparison among the mean scores further suggested that there was a tendency of increase in home assignment value from class 6th to class 7th, but after that it had a tendency of decrease (The mean score of class 8th students was lower in comparison to that of class 7th, which was higher than the mean score of class 6th). This pattern of increase followed by a decrease across class 6th, 7th and 8th was visible on other work value variables also. Although, the mean differences were not significant at appropriate statistical level (The F-value associated with mean differences on 'total work value' was 2.58 and was significant at .10 level only); but it draws attention, particularly because the pattern seemed to be interesting and significant for elementary schooling. Certainly it needs further elaboration to assess the validity of the pattern, and also to know the possible reasons of such decline in students' work values after class 7th.

Table 2.4 : Comparison among Students of Classes 6th, 7th and 8th on Work Values (N for each Class was 80).

Variables	*Class 6th Mean (SD)*	*Class 7th Mean (SD)*	*Class 8th Mean (SD)*	*F-value*
Domestic Work Value	21.80 (2.06)	22.33 (1.69)	22.02 (2.40)	1.29
Knowledge through Work	20.15 (1.14)	20.05 (1.65)	20.23 (1.75)	0.26
Positive Feelings with Works	14.53 (2.16)	14.98 (1.76)	14.68 (1.73)	1.17
Home Assignment Value	14.80 (2.06)	15.80 (2.06)	15.20 (2.06)	5.87**
Total Work Value	68.70 (5.16)	70.40 (4.06)	69.48 (4.95)	2.58

Note: ** $p < .01$

At this stage, it can be concluded that the results, based on examination of significance of mean differences indicated that gender played more significant role. The female students were found to have higher work values in comparison to their male classmates.

Interestingly, they did not differ with each other on domestic work value and home assignment value. The rural and urban students also did not differ on these two factors, but they showed patterns of differences on the rest of scores. Rural people had more positive feelings with works, whereas the scores on the knowledge through works were higher in urban students. The grades of the students also were found determining the variations in work values. The scores on the work values obtained in case of class 7th students were higher than that of class 6th, suggesting an improvement in work values at this stage. However, the scores of class 8th students were either not different with the scores of class 7th students, or were relatively lower. It indicated a possibility of stagnation in development of work values after class 7th. This can be regarded to be a serious point to be attended properly.

Interaction Effects

It was also planned to evaluate the effects of interactions among three independent variables that is gender, rural-urban habitation and schooling grades on variations in work values of students. In order to do this, the method of analysis of variance was used to analyze the data placed in a 2×2×3 design (2 types of sexes, 2 types of habitations, and 3 grades of schooling or classes). The Table 2.5 presents F-values obtained for the main effects and interaction effects of independent variables on different indices of work values.

The findings regarding the main effects of the three independent variables on indices of work values, as is available in Table 2.5, need not any further elaboration; as it were naturally similar to the findings of t-tests and one way analysis of variance that are already reported earlier. Among the interaction effects, the effects of interaction between gender and rural-urban habitation were found to be significant on only two indices of work values namely; 'knowledge through work' and 'home assignment value'. The significance level was only .05 in both the cases.

The effects of interaction between gender and schooling grades was significant on domestic work value ($F = 3.75$, $p < .05$), home assignment value ($F = 7.83$, $p < .01$), and total work value ($F = 5.16$, $p < .01$). This interaction did not affect significantly 'knowledge through work', and 'positive feelings with works'. The Table 2.5 further reveals that the interaction effect of rural-urban habitation

Table 2.5: F-Values, denoting Main and Interaction Effects of Gender, Rural-Urban Habitation and Schooling Grades on Indices of Work Values

Independent Variables	*Domestic Work Value*	*Knowledge through Work*	*Positive Feeling with works*	*Home Assignment Value*	*Total Work Value*
Main Effects					
1. Gender	0.58	12.15**	7.83**	0.52	6.82**
2. Habitation	0.78	2.88	14.45**	0.33	1.74
3. Grades	1.33	0.30	1.30	6.28**	2.74
Interaction Effects					
1. Gender *Habitation	2.30	4.22*	3.22	4.65*	0.66
2. Gender *Grades	3.75*	1.46	2.66	7.83**	5.16**
3. Habitation *Grades	1.87	1.97	1.63	1.01	1.08
4. Gender * Habitation *Grades	0.25	7.10**	0.39	1.18	1.22

Note: * $p < .05$, ** $p < .01$

and schooling grades was not significant on any of indices of work values. However, the effect of interaction among gender, rural-urban habitation and schooling grades was significant only on one index of work value. This index was 'knowledge through work' ($F = 7.10$, $p < .01$). On the rest of indices, this interaction effect was not significant.

It has been a tradition to use method of graphical representation to demonstrate the pattern of significant interaction effects. In this method the graphs are plotted using mean scores of cells of the factorial table—developed on the basis of different factors of independent variables. The same has been done in the present report also.

The mean scores necessary to represent the significant effects of interaction between gender and rural-urban habitation graphically, are reported in Table 2.6. The SDs are also given with the means for the convenience of better comprehension of the interaction effects.

From the effects of interactions among these three variables, only one interaction effect (between gender and class) was significant.

The female students of class 6 and 7 scored higher in comparison to their mail counterparts. Such difference was not obtained among class 8th students. It also suggested above said stagnation after class 7th.

Table 2.6: Means and Standard Deviations (for Significant 'Gender*Habitation')

	Knowledge through Work		*Home Assignment Value*	
	Boys Mean (SD)	*Girls Mean (SD)*	*Boys Mean (SD)*	*Girls Mean (SD)*
Rural	19.47 (2.25)	20.50 (0.68)	15.50 (1.85)	15.17 (2.12)
Urban	20.17 (1.22)	20.43 (1.34)	14.87 (1.98)	15.53 (1.56)

On the basis of means, appearing in Table 2.6, two graphs (Fig. 2.1 and Fig. 2.2) were plotted.

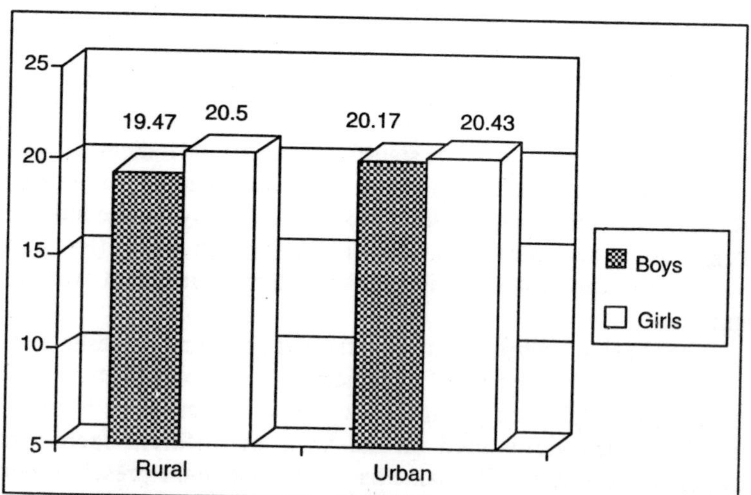

Fig. 2.1: Effect of Gender × Rural-urban Habitation on Scores on Knowledge through Work

Fig. 2.1 represents the effect of interaction between gender and rural-urban habitation on 'knowledge through work', which was one index of work values. As is evident from the figure, girls scored higher on this index of work value in comparison to the boys, in rural and urban—both residential habitation conditions. It suggests that the girls value work because, according to them, it provides knowledge. Some of the earlier studies have indicated that in comparison to boys, the girls are more willing to learn as much as possible, in order to enhance their knowledge. This result supports it once again. Further, the urban boys scored little higher than the rural boys on this index. Since, the rural-urban distinction was not found among girls, therefore, it can be postulated that the rural-urban habitation affects the work values of boys but not of girls.

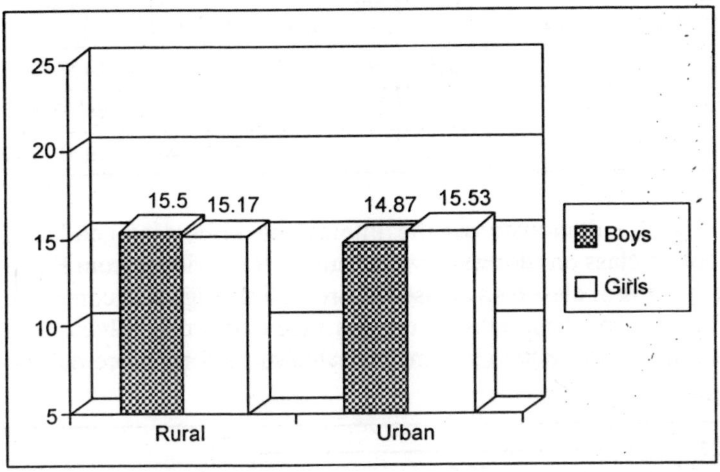

Fig. 2.2: Effect of Gender × Rural-Urban Habitation on Scores on Home Assignment Value

The rural-urban habitation affects the work values of boys but not of girls—it was visible in Fig. 2.2 also. This figure presents the effect of interaction between gender and rural-urban habitation on 'home assignment value', which was another index of work values. On this index the rural boys scored higher in comparison to urban boys. In fact, the urban boys were found to have least home assignment value, while urban girls had highest home assignment value. It seems to suggest that the boys' values need more attention, particularly in urban area. In rural areas, the boys had little greater home assignment value in comparison to the girls.

The Table 2.7 presents means and standard deviations for significant effects of interaction between gender and schooling class.

On the basis of the means of this table, Figs. 2.3, 2.4 and 2.5 are plotted.

Table 2.7: Means and Standard Deviations (for significant 'Gender* Schooling* Class').

Indices of work values		*Class 6 Mean (SD)*	*Class 7 Mean (SD)*	*Class 8 Mean (SD)*
Domestic Work Value	*Boys*	21.30 (2.68)	22.15 (1.70)	22.40 (1.74)
	Girls	22.30 (0.97)	22.50 (1.68)	21.65 (2.89)
Home Assignment Value	*Boys*	14.10 (2.49)	15.85 (1.67)	15.60 (1.41)
	Girls	15.50 (1.30)	15.75 (1.69)	14.80 (2.34)
Total Work Value	*Boys*	66.70 (6.12)	69.75 (3.20)	69.80 (4.47)
	Girls	70.70 (2.87)	71.05 (4.71)	69.15 (5.42)

Fig. 2.3 demonstrates the interaction effects of gender and schooling class on 'domestic work value'. It is evident from Fig. 2.3 that the girls of class 6 and class 7 scored a little higher in comparison to the boys of these classes on this index of work values. In the community, where the girls are expected to perform more domestic

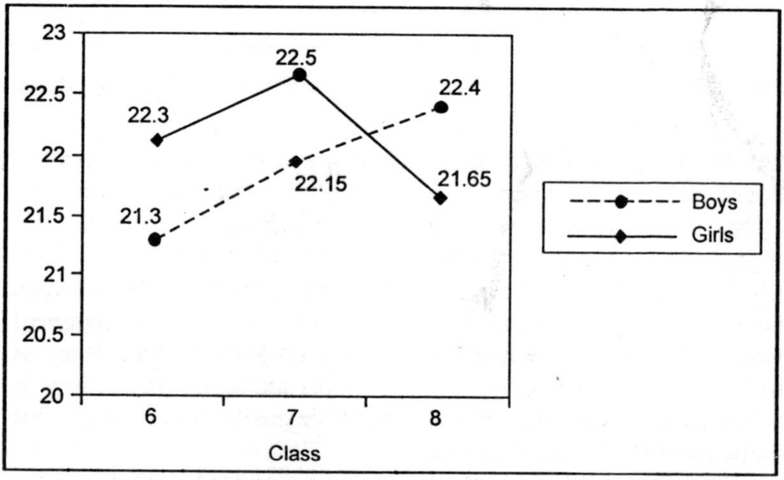

Fig. 2.3: Effect of Gender × Class on Scores on Domestic Work Value

works, this result seems to be as per expectation. However, the mean score of girls of class 8 were lower in comparison to the mean scores of girls of class 6 and class 7. It suggested the tendency of decline in domestic work value among the girls after class 7. This tendency was not seen among boys.

The tendency of decline in work values among girls after class 7 is visible in Fig. 2.4 and Fig. 2.5 also. The Fig. 2.4 is plotted for the effects of interaction between gender and schooling classes on 'home assignment value'. This figure tells that the girls of class 6 had more home assignment value than the boys of their class. There was no difference between the boys and the girls in class 7th. In class 8th, the pattern was just reverse to that of class 6th. In this class, the girls were found to have lower home assignment value in comparison to the boys of this class. These findings can be treated to be significant, particularly from the point of view of sex difference in the variations in work values across different schooling classes. Also, the increase in home assignment value among boys and decrease in this index of work values among girls during their advancement from class 6th to class 8th may draw attention of researchers in this area.

Fig. 2.5 presents the pattern of the interaction effect of gender and schooling classes on the 'total work value'. It reveals that the

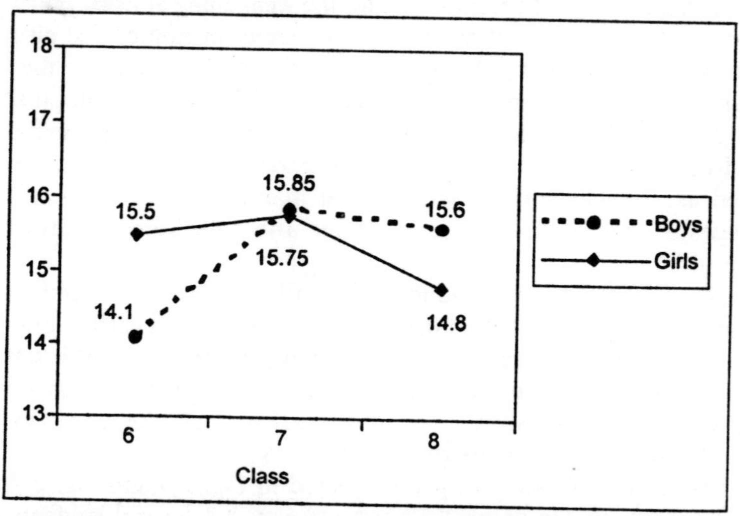

Fig. 2.4: Effect of Gender × Class on Scores on Home Assignment Value

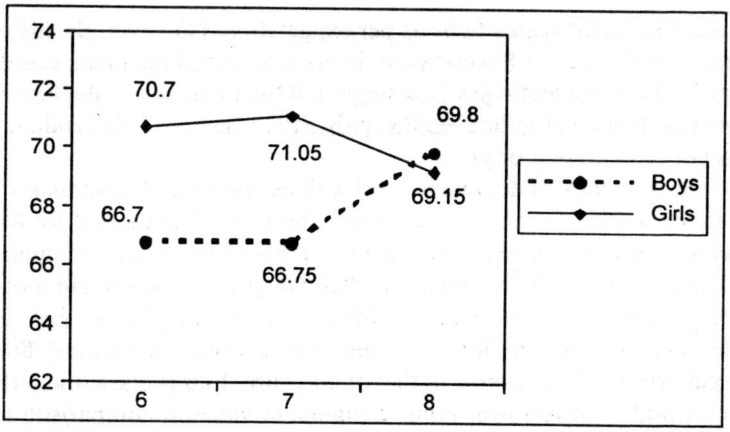

Fig. 2.5: Effect of Gender × Class on Scores on Total Work Value

girls of class 6th and class 7th scored higher on this index of work values than their male classmates. But at class 8th level no difference was found between boys and girls. It appears that the work values among girls get drastically transformed at the class 8th level. More often the work values among girls weaken at this level. However, it does not happen among the boys of this class. It necessitates to trace the factors that might be responsible for the weakening of work values among girl students of class 8th in some study in future. The girls entering in class 8th are 13 to 15 years old. During this age they begin with several types of external and internal physiological changes, which have acute psychological impacts on their mental build-up. Thus one research question for some future study can be raised as: To what extent and in what manner the physiological changes in girls of 13 to15 years of age affect the work values of these girls?

The effects of interactions among all the three independent variables were also tested by using ANOVA. As is told earlier, only one interaction effect was found to be significant. It was the effect of interaction among gender, habitation and schooling class on 'Knowledge Through Work'. The means and standard deviations for this interaction effect is reported in Table 2.8.

The means of Table 2.8 are presented in Fig. 2.6 and Fig. 2.7. Fig. 2.6 contains the graph for boys and Fig. 2.7 for girl students. These figures suggest that the rural-urban habitation affected the

Table 2.8: Means and Standard Deviations on 'Knowledge Through Work' (for 'Gender*Habitation*Schooling Class').

		Class 6 Mean (SD)	*Class 7* Mean (SD)	*Class 8* Mean (SD)
Boys	*Rural*	20.10 (0.97)	19.20 (2.19)	19.10 (3.06)
	Urban	19.30 (1.52)	20.70 (0.66)	20.50 (0.83)
Girls	*Rural*	20.40 (0.68)	20.40 (0.68)	20.70 (0.66)
	Urban	20.80 (0.62)	19.90 (2.07)	20.60 (0.68)

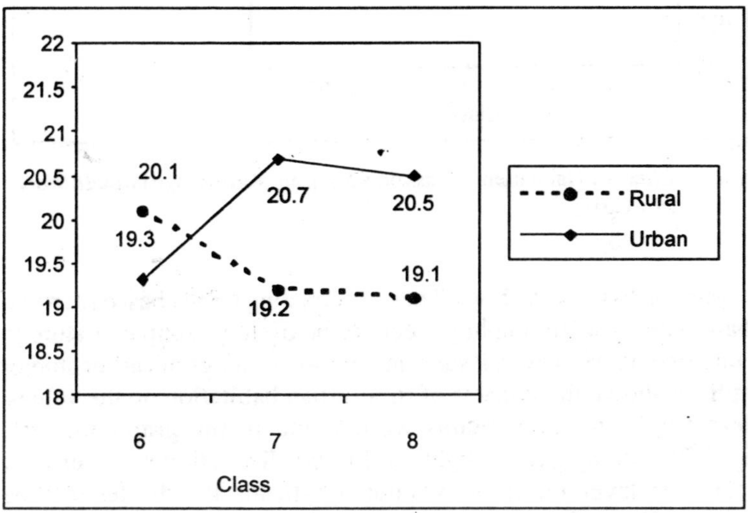

Fig. 2.6: Effect of Habitation × Class on Scores on 'Knowledge through Works' (for Boys)

scores on 'knowledge through works' more in boys. In all the three classes the rural boys differed with urban boys on this factor of work value, but the pattern of difference was not similar. There was a declining tendency in the graph, obtained for rural boys on this factor between class 6th and class 7th; whereas the graph for urban boys had an upward trend at the same levels. It resulted the great difference between rural and urban boys on this index of work values at the level of class 8th. Thus the urban boys of this class appeared to have significantly higher value for 'knowledge through works' in

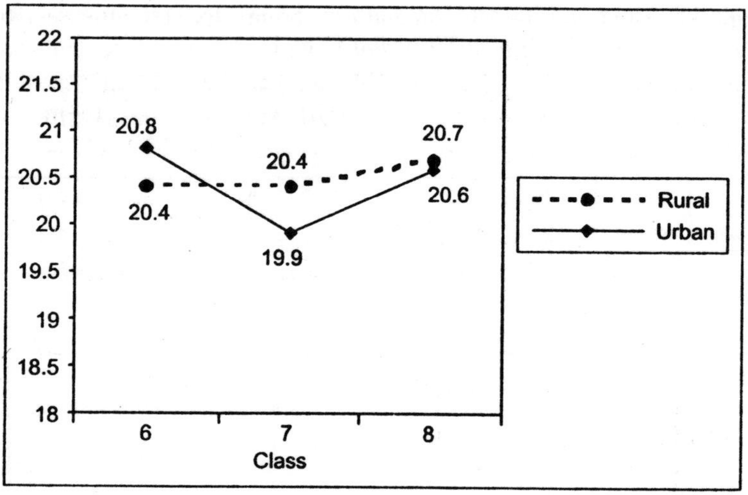

Fig. 2.7: Effect of Habitation × Class on Scores on 'Knowledge through Works' (for Girls)

comparison to the rural boys. These contrasting trends based on rural-urban distinction among boys seem to be of very complex nature to be understood. However, it substantiates the findings of earlier studies that have shown the impacts of rural-urban habitation on the values. Interestingly, no such trends were found in the graph for girls (Fig. 2.7). Among girls, a slight rural-urban distinction was seen only at class 7th level, but it too was not significant. It indicates that the possible affects of external and internal physiological changes in girls on their work values of this age group, as was hypothesized earlier in this section, were not visible at this stage.

A Conclusive Overview of the Results

Chapter 2 is an important part of the present project report, as it has presented the detailed particulars about the planning, procedure and findings of the study that was conducted in the project. The study was not of empirical nature only, it was of explanatory nature as well. Therefore, both quantitative and qualitative statistical methods were applied in the study. It yielded a number of results having significant implications.

The findings of phase 1 revealed that there are very few references of relevant work related themes in the textbooks of Hindi, English and Social Studies of 6th, 7th and 8th classes. Even the themes, that were available in these text-books, were not presented in some impressive manners, so as to be able to affect the children's opinions regarding work, or to instil the work values among them. The information, obtained in phase 2, suggested that there was conscientious opinions among students, parents and teachers about the children's feelings about work. According to them, the children not only understand the meaning of work, they know the importance, benefits and other implications of doing works, also. These stakeholders further opined that the present education system is responsible for the poor work values among the students. The results of these two phases supported the findings of several earlier studies conducted in this area, some of which are referred in the review of literature—presented in Chapter 1 of this report. On the basis of important findings of these studies, it has been frequently suggested to make modifications in the present education system. Certainly, while doing so, the text-books also would require modification.

The phase 3 was the major part of the project. In this phase, first of all, data were collected from 240 students of class 6th, 7th and 8th. Half number of these students were boys and the rest half were girls. Similarly, half of them were from rural areas, while the other half were from urban areas. The obtained data were statistically analyzed, first with the objective to develop a reliable and valid scale of work values for Jr. High School students; and further to examine the roles of some contextual variables on variations in work values among these students.

The work value scale for Jr. High School was developed on the basis of four factors of work values that appeared as the significant factors from the factor analysis of data. The four factors were; domestic work value, knowledge through work, positive feelings with works, and home assignment value. Thus the final scale contained four different sub-scales for the four factors. The scores, obtained on these sub-scales were added to develop a composite score for total work value. The successful development of a work value scale for Jr. High School students on the basis of scientifically investigated four factors of work values provided rationales to the operationalization of work value in the context of elementary education, which was earlier questioned by the experts during the elementary planning of the present project. The nature of four factors, emerged as the significant factors of work values from the data obtained from the children studying in Jr. High School classes, seemed to substantiate the presumption—presented in the beginning of this section of the present report, according to which the work values of the students of elementary level might be operationalized in terms of attributes such as, likelihood to accept and owning the works or assignments, perception of desirability of work, love for the works and enjoyment in doing it, ability to distinguish between work and non-work, sharing the feelings of parents about work, and evaluation of instrumentality of works to achieve the desired objectives.

Several work value scale are available in the industrial and organizational academic areas, but only a few scale for measuring work values among children have been developed. The qualification of present developed scale is its applicability in the specific context of students of Jr. High School students.

The examination of variations in work values across the contextual variables (gender, rural-urban habitation, and classes or grades of the students) revealed that among the three variables, gender appeared to be most potent determinant of work values among these students. In review section, several researches have been reviewed, which have established the significant role of gender in determining work values. However, since the focus of the present proposal is transformation of work value, therefore, the contentions of Lindsay and Knox (1984) draw special attention here. They had concluded from their research findings that gender is a major influence that should be included in models of work value change. It is not that gender is directly related to work value change; rather, gender is related to the initial work values to educational attainment and most strongly to the extrinsic job characteristic, income. Male preference for the extrinsic work value and female preference for the intrinsic work value reflects, perhaps, traditional gender role differentiation.

Gender has been universally found significant determinants of many of the social, educational and psychological processes in most of the studies, conducted in different background of national identities. (In a recent study based on survey of more than five thousand people of U.K., it was found that in comparison to men, more number of women have a feeling of pleasure in life. *Dainik Jagaran,* Lucknow, 11th April, 2010). Although the activists of feminist movements would hesitate to agree but it is a fact that there are natural differences between males and females on various physiological and psychological grounds. However, the systems including the educational system of a civilized society need to work to check the probabilities of gender-based discrimination in the society due to these differences. The findings of the present study of work value can be explored to get relevant cues applicable in this context.

The rural-urban habitation and the classes (6th, 7th and 8th) were found to determine work value up to only limited extents. However, a tendency of stagnation or a little declination in different factors of work values during the development from 6th standard to 8th standard was noticed. It was really a matter of worry, and was suggestive for a careful investigation on this issue.

3

Policy Implications

The project was planned with the ambition that after its completion the project would yield relevant information, useful in producing concrete suggestions for reform in curriculum of elementary level of education, which would be consequently helpful in instilling positive work values among the students of this level. Also, it was expected that the findings of the study would be utilizable for the purpose of providing suggestions and guidelines for teachers and parents, which they might use in nurturing the work values of their children. Since the project is completed now and its findings are presented in the final report, therefore, one can move forward to finally assess the implications of the results of the project.

The results of the project, in general, have supported the necessity of reform in present educational system. As has been reported earlier, there is a general consensus among policy-makers, researchers of the area and planners on this point (e.g., Neumann and Neumann, 1983; Pandian, 2005; Naike, 2008). Venkataraman (2007) emphasized to start this reform from the elementary level of education. The findings of study presented in this report seem to substantiate this view by providing evidences in support of necessity of reform at Jr. High School level.

One must concede that different aspects of human civilization change with time. It is inevitable and it cannot be stopped. These changes pose threats and challenges before the existing educational system in all the times, because due to these changes, every time phase demands differently from the education system. This has been clearly elaborated by Rodgers (1980) in very logical manner. (The arguments of Rodgers are presented in detail in chapter 1 of this report). Now, it is twenty-first century. Several surveys have indicated that the children of this century are facing problems of new nature (Achenbach and Howell, 1993). Thus it is the responsibility of the educational system of modern era to equip these children with the capabilities, required to cope with the problems of the era. The educational system can fulfil this responsibility only after critically reviewing its present format to find out its limitations in the context of new century, and also by enriching itself with new supplements to enhance its scope to match with the special requirements of this century. The findings of different studies conducted in recent years in the related areas can be explored to develop such supplements.

The complexity of the challenges before the children of today was well noticed by Garbarino (1998), when he exclaimed 'How difficult it is to grow up (for children) these days!'. He analyzed the data and results of study by Achenbach and Howell (1993), which had conclusively suggested that 'more and more (American) children were in greater and greater trouble' on emotional and behavioural fronts. Garbarino felt that it was due to the increasingly socially toxic environment. Garbarino offered the term of 'socially toxic environment' as a parallel to the environmental movement's analysis regarding physical toxicity as the threat to human well-being and survival. Serious concerns regarding negative consequences of increase of toxic substances in the physical environment—in the air, in the water and in the soil, have been frequently expressed. But the toxicities of social environment are not less dangerous. Although everyone is vulnerable to toxicity in the social environment, children (like the elderly) are the most vulnerable, just as they are among the most vulnerable to physical toxicity in the environment. Therefore, the children should be guarded against physical as well as social toxicity. Also they should be equipped with the capabilities to guard themselves. Here, the government and society have major role to play. Garbarino finally suggests developing sound foundation for educating children which might focus positively on what children need to thrive, and to channel its efforts into realizing that vision. It would demand active interventions in existing educational system.

Before focusing on the policy implications of the findings of present project, it seems to make clear that the study was not only of empirical nature, it was explanatory as well. The qualitative and quantitative—both types of statistical techniques were used in the project. Both of these techniques have limitations and the results should be comprehended under the restrictions of these limitations. There has been mixed types of opinions particularly about the findings of quantitative techniques. Some strong critics of heavily reliance on standardized statistical procedures in most of the studies in social sciences call the findings, obtained from these procedures 'merely the numerical jargons', but others believe that these findings are valid and significantly contribute to the knowledge in the respective areas. These findings draw attention to the possible answers of the problems, raise new hunches or research questions, and suggest the possible strategy of interventions in the problematic situations. With the assumption that the latter opinion has sound ground, the attempts have been made to take the indications of the findings of the present study to suggest following policy implications.

Correction in Present Education System

The findings and the conclusions, that have been drawn from these findings unequivocally confirm that the present education system needs modification, and this modification should start from the level of elementary education. In Phase 2, it was found that about 63 per cent of the stakeholders, including students, teachers and parents believed that if the students of Jr. High School level lack the understanding of meaning and importance of work, it is due to the fault of our education system. The specific suggestion from the findings is to enrich the text-books of this level with the themes that could develop adequate attitudes and values regarding work among the students. It would certainly require the modification in curricula to be taught at this level.

The present era is 'era of professionalism'. In this context, the present education system has more often adopted the curricula with restricted objective to develop professional skills among students. However, in these curricula, the professional skill is meant as the strictly scientific knowledge—applicable to get employment or some other means of money making. This meaning represents only one side of professional skills. Therefore, the present education system is bringing one sided development among the students, and it seems that due to such one sided development the students are failing to prove their worth to be successful and responsible citizens of society or nation in future.

Patil (2008) has stated that 'achievement of an individual in any field of activity depends on the levels of skills, the person has acquired. It also depends on the attitudes, understanding, decisiveness and values with which the individual acts'. This statement clearly recognize that the professional skill of more inclusive nature is required for the achievements. Therefore, the education system should broaden its scope to teach professional skill of broader nature, which combines the scientific skill with progressive attitudes, values and understandings. Such type of teaching would be instrumental for the wholistic development of the students that would relate occupational skills with the better human qualities. For this purpose, the education system needs correction.

We Indians are frequently said to be lazy and work-shirking people. Therefore, in our context, the progressive work values should be regarded to be an important part of comprehensive nature of professional skills—to be taught through our educational system. The specific focus of present project is on generating work values among the students of elementary level. In this context, following corrective measures can be suggested on the basis of results of the project.

1. First and foremost important measure in this regard would be modification at curricula level. Patil (2008) has expressed the view that the school curriculum should contain components that communicate essential values in their totality. The results of the project suggest that in the curriculum at Jr. High School level, the number of work related themes or references are very few. It should be increased. Although there are some themes related to work in the text-books of this level, but in these references also, the implications of work or work value are referred in very superficial manner, having no significant impacts on students. For example, Mahatma Gandhi's biography and his struggle for freedom are available in text-books, but his views on 'work', which are quite motivating, are not highlighted anywhere. Similarly, the slogan of '*Aram Haram Hai*' is available but its contextual and practical relevance is not discussed. The policy-makers should act to fill such gaps. It can be further advised to include the dedicated and energetic works of legendary personalities of modern era; such as that of Abul Kalam in the text-books. Also, the schools should

include the practical work in the fields and extension lectures by experts in their curricula, relevant for the purpose.

2. The parents, teachers and administrative staff concede that the students cannot be blamed for not having proper work values. It is due to failure of entire education system. As the corrective measures, the teachers should be given special training of instilling work values among their students. As can be recalled here, many voices have been raised suggesting teachers to work hard in order to cultivate and promote values among students (Pandian, 2005; Nnaike, 2008). Also, the parents should be provided suggestions and guidelines—useful in nurturing the work values of their children at guardians meet. The teachers and the parents should act jointly to encourage the students to answer for themselves: What do they want to be? What are their capabilities to do this?, and What do they want to be known for? It can be believed that the answers of such questions would automatically relate with the work values of these students. The curricula should be reframed to be able to give the students the opportunities to focus on these questions.

Meaning of Work for Children : Some Corrective Suggestions

The findings of Phase 2 of the project revealed that the group of students, teachers, parents and administrative staff, who were interviewed in this phase, believed that the children studying at Jr. High School level understand the meaning of work. However, they mean it more in physical term such as, homework, obeying the elders of the family, responsibility or as the domestic works. According to them, these children would prefer to work such tasks in future that would provide them money or other physical benefits including the name and fame. Obviously these findings suggest that the children recognize the instrumental nature of work. Perhaps they do not have idea of intrinsic approach to work. In the intrinsic approach the work itself, is regarded to be enjoyable. The children need to be made them aware about the intrinsic benefits of the works also. As has been discussed in the review section, the benefits of work is not restricted to that of only extrinsic nature. The work is beneficial from social, psychological, physiological and some more points of views. It provides satisfaction, recognition, opportunity of social contacts, physiological strength, and a shaped body. Here it seems relevant to refer a call by first lady of USA, Michel Obama. She announced on 9th February, 2010 her new initiative called 'Let Us Move' to combat childhood obesity. Mrs. Obama was perturbed by the report, according to which obesity is plaguing in every 1 in 3 American children. She suggested the parents, teachers and other related persons to focus on work and sense of responsibility among children, and to make them busy in a variety of works. Then they would have less time sitting in front of TV and being more prone for obesity (Retrieved www.myjobchart.com/my-job-chart/teaching-kids-to-work/12.2.2010). Indian children are also showing obesity in large number. They also can be taught this point to modify the meaning of work for them.

There has been a confusion that the intrinsic and extrinsic work values are the two opposite poles of a single dimension, therefore, it is assumed that an enhancement in one type of work value would cause a decrement in the other type of value. The findings of studies have contradicted it. For example, Mortimer, *et al.* (1996), on the basis of the results of their empirical studies suggested that many adolescents who had higher intrinsic orientations were also the more extrinsically oriented. This point should be seriously noted by teachers and parents. They should attempt to implant it in the mind of the children also

Although the intrinsic aspects of work have been frequently advocated in Indian religious and philosophical traditions, many of the adults of our society also do not show interests in the intrinsic approach to work. In *Srimad Bhagwad Gita*, to work with a sense of non-attachment (*Anasakti*) is strongly advocated. Here the non-attachment does not mean detachment from the work (Naidu and Pandey, 1992). Rather it means to work without being heavily concerned with the 'specific' rewards from the work. It should be believed that any work would necessarily follow with some kind of reward, either just after the completion of the work or later in future. Also, the reward may not be necessarily that 'specific' as was desired. It can be in different form. Therefore, one should work and have faith in this law. Suppose that a student did not succeed in his competitive examination despite his hard and dedicated study, he should not feel frustration or sense of failure. He should feel that he is now more prepared for his second attempt in that examination. In the context of above arguments, it seems advisable to intervene to modify the meanings of work among children just by making them aware to the possibility of 'work with a sense of non-attachment'. It can be developed as a skill (Tiwari, 2000). This skill would check the tension and frustration among these children, which are proving to have disastrous impacts on these children—sometimes resulting the tendency of suicide among them.

The findings of the present study revealed that the children define work in limited manner. They have shown, more often, a negative attitude towards work. They are not aware of the multifarious benefits of a work. Here is the need of interventions. The curriculum and socialization processes should aim to train the children to be able to comprehend the meaning of work in broader sense. They should be aware of different positive aspects of work, and should develop with a favourable attitudes towards work.

Work Values in Children : Measurement and Variations

In this project, a reliable and valid scale to measure the work value in children have been developed. It contained four sub-scales, one for each of four factors of work values. These factors had emerged as the significant factors during the factor analysis of data obtained in the project. The four factors were named as domestic work value, knowledge through work, positive feelings with works, and home assignment value. These factors substantiated the stand that the work values among children of Jr. High School standards can be operationalized and measured.

It can be believed that the new scale can be used to assess the work values among students in order to educate them adequately. The administering of this scale itself might suggest the children 'indirectly' to improve their work values. After administering it, the results can be discussed among the teachers and parents to chalk out strategies for instilling the appropriate work values among the students. Also, the results can be utilized to give the students 'direct' suggestions for the betterment of their future.

As far as the variations in work values of children was concerned, it was found in the results that the gender was most potent determinant of the variation. The rural-urban habitation affected it in only few cases. These findings can be utilized in the attempts of eradicating the gender or habitation based discrimination in society. It is an unfortunate fact that the social groups, particularly the family, itself teaches different patterns of work values for its male and female children. Therefore, it seems that the educational system has to play 'double' role in this situation. It has to correct the erroneous teachings of family and other social communities at one hand, and to inculcate appropriate work values among children at the other hand. However, one should be honest to accept that the eradication of variations in work values across different factors is not very easy. That is why that the researchers have advised the counsellors to recognize the possibilities of these variations while working for vocational counselling (Leong and Tata, 1990).

One possible impact of schooling grades (class 6th, 7th and 8th) sought special attention. There were evidences suggesting either a stagnation or a declination in work values after class 7th. It seems that the new studies—focusing on this special hunch—are required and if in these studies also the similar results are found, it would necessitate to seriously trace the causes for the failure of development of work values after class 7th. Also, serious attempts would be needed to eradicate these causes.

The Notion of 'Crystallized India' and Work Value

It is a common saying that 'the real India' lives in villages. Does it signify that city dwellers represent an 'artificial India'? The phrase 'artificial India' may seem nonsense but it gets reasonable sense in the widely accepted idea of two types of India. It is a fact that a large number of Indians, particularly of urban area, have received a highly westernized education and have formed a new class in India. Pt. Jawahar Lal Nehru had recognized this new class early in 1964 and had written: The British had formed a new class in India—English educated class, which lived in a world of its own, cut off from the masses of population and looked always toward its rulers (*The Discovery of India*, pp. 413-414). It is thus apparent that the westernized education has widened the gap between the two types of India.

The proponents of the 'theory of two India' distinguish between the two types of India on the basis of several criteria. The critical review of opinions of different scholars seems to suggest that along with other criteria, the two types of India can be differentiated on the basis of 'attitude towards poverty' also. As has been discussed earlier, a majority of Indian people, primarily of rural India, is contended even in their miserably poor economic conditions. Segal (1966) had seen it as a uniqueness of poverty in India. There has been a sense of general satisfaction and acceptance of *status quo*, i.e., whatever is ordained through the fate would be automatically attained and beyond that can never be achieved. According to Sinha (1999), 'such rationalization tends to generate an attitude of acceptance of imperfect human conditions without a desire to modify, master or improve—it inculcates fatalism and get reflected in people's acceptance of the *status quo*.' This thinking is well expressed in popular exclamations like; *Jehi Bidhi Rakhe Ram Tehi Bidhi Rahie* (Live as prescribed by Lord Ram). Palsane and Lam (1996) had also noted this attitude and opined that under the influence of religion, Indian society had become fatalistic, complacent and stagnant. According to them, such attitudes acted as obstacles to economic and technological development.

In contrast to these people, the above stated 'new class' of people in India has rather different kind of attitudes. As stated earlier, they have attained the westernized education. This type of education puts emphasis on science and technology. The people, educated in this tradition, utilized their scientific and technological knowledge in money making to improve their financial status. It paved the path of their material development. However, it followed with some negative consequences also. In fact these people, influenced by general observations prevalent in our country about the acute scarcity of resources, soon felt unsecured and developed a belief that they or their children might lose what they have and become poor at some stage. With this belief they engaged themselves in acquiring, hoarding, and monopolizing more and more resources (J.B.P. Sinha, 2008). Using the terminology developed by J.B.P. Sinha (1977 a), one can say that they suffered from a 'poverty syndrome', which has been conceptualized as a fear of poverty even in the minds of those who are not-so-poor. It can be assumed that the noticeable increase in black marketing, hoarding and earning through foul means is attributable to such attitudes and beliefs.

Obviously, both types of attitudes are detrimental for the required development of the country and its people. It leads to assume that both types of India lack pro-development attributes. It does not bar the national development only, but damage the prospects of human development in the country, also. J.B.P. Sinha (1977, b) had rightly argued that extreme poverty dehumanizes a person while too much of material affluence desensitizes him to others—both are detrimental to human development. He had proposed that moderation in economic achievement and inclusion of human values were the essence of human development.

The similar opinion was expressed by the author of this book, in his one of earlier articles (Tiwari, 2007). The article had described the different sets of attitudinal components and other factors of belief system associated with the two types of India that were creating hindrances in the all-round development of the country despite of the many ambitious schemes launched by governments and other organizations. Also, this article suggested the need of specific transformations of social-psychological attributes of the people of so-called 'the real India' or 'the artificial India' in order to build a new real development oriented India. In the article, a new notion as 'Crystallized India' was presented to identify such a transformed India.

The development of India as a 'Crystallized India' would certainly need the inculcation of adequate work values among the people of the country alongwith the transformations of their other types of attitudinal and belief-related attributes. Ultimately we have a need to remove the label of being a believer in '*Aram*' culture. We will have to emerge as the hard workers. Then only we will be able to provide the nation a 'human capital of great qualities'. It is not that the policy makers of our country have not recognized these facts. They have been always advocating for proactive approaches in this direction. The study and its results, reported in this book, may prove to be helpful for them in their planning to use the education system for this purpose. Particularly, they can explore the prospects of using the curricula development for the different levels of education including that of elementary level in their endeavours.

Limitations of the Study

The scientific approach suggests that the findings of any study should be comprehended with the awareness of possible limitations of the study. The study, reported in this dissertation, also had certain limitations. Therefore, the findings of the study should be interpreted taking these limitations under considerations.

This report contains the detailed description of an empirical study along with the theoretical interpretations of issues associated with the work values among children. The area of work value (even in the limited context of children) is very broad. Although, the theoretical interpretations have tried to focus on the broad and comprehensive nature of work values in children, but the empirical part of the study was restricted to that of children, studying at Junior High School level. The size of the sample also was small. Therefore, any generalization on the basis of findings of this study would need necessary precautions. In this study, a scale for measuring work values among school-going children is developed. Its reliability and validity is claimed on the basis of data of present study. However, since the sample size was not appropriately sufficient in this study, therefore, the reliability and validity of developed scale are still questionable. It is advised to verify it through the data of a large sample before using the scale in some new study.

The study, presented in this report, was limited to bring into focus the significance of children's works from different angles. Also, it highlighted the necessity of interventions for the purpose of inculcation of positive work values among children. It is advocated that such interventions would need the educational reforms, including the modifications in curriculum. Now the educationists and policy makers have responsibility to take it into their consideration and act accordingly.

APPENDIX-A

मनोवैज्ञानिक अध्ययन

महोदय,

हम एक मनोवैज्ञानिक अध्ययन में आपका सहयोग चाहते हैं। इस अध्ययन में जूनियर हाई स्कूल (कक्षा 8 तक) के विद्यार्थियों के 'कार्य' (Work) के बारे में समझ तथा धारणा का आकलन किया जायेगा। आपके समक्ष कुछ प्रश्न प्रस्तुत किये जायेंगे जिनका सम्बन्ध कार्य के विषय में इन बच्चों के विचारों से होगा। इन प्रश्नों के उत्तर आप खुल कर दे सकते हैं, किन्तु यह ध्यान में रखियेगा कि आप क्या सोचते हैं।–यह नहीं बताना है, बल्कि जूनियर हाई स्कूल का विद्यार्थी कैसा सोचता होगा–आपको इसका अनुमान करते हुए प्रश्न का उत्तर देना है।

आप के सहयोग के लिए हम आभारी रहेंगे।

सादर,

(डॉ. ए. के. तिवारी)
रीडर, मनोविज्ञान,
का. सु. साकेत स्नातकोत्तर महाविद्यालय
अयोध्या, फैजाबाद

नाम : ....विद्यार्थी/शिक्षक/अभिवावक

आयु : ....

व्यवसाय : ....

संस्था : ....

जूनियर हाई स्कूल तक
के पाल्यों की संख्या : ....

क्रमशः

- आप के विचार से क्या जूनियर हाई स्कूल (कक्षा 8 तक) के बच्चे कार्य अथवा काम अथवा work का मतलब समझते हैं? हाँ/नहीं
  यदि हाँ तो क्या समझते हैं, यदि नहीं तो क्यों नहीं समझते?

- क्या उन्हें काम का मतलब समझना चाहिये? यदि हाँ, तो किस अर्थ में?

- काम या कार्य अनेक प्रकार के होते हैं जैसे—शारीरिक श्रम पर आधारित कार्य या मानसिक श्रम पर आधारित कार्य, इत्यादि। ऐसे कुछ कार्यों के नाम बताइये?

- जो कार्य आपने बताये हैं उन्हें जूनियर हाई स्कूल तक के विद्यार्थियों की पसन्दगी के आधार पर किस क्रम में रखा जा सकता है? अर्थात्, विद्यार्थी जिसे सबसे अधिक पसन्द करते होंगे उन्हें पहले स्थान पर, उससे कम पसन्द के कार्यों को दूसरे स्थान पर तथा इस प्रकार क्रमबद्ध करिये।

- जूनियर हाई स्कूल तक के विद्यार्थियों को किस प्रकार के कार्य कराये जाने चाहिए?

- काम या कार्य करने से क्या-क्या लाभ हैं? क्या जूनियर हाई स्कूल के विद्यार्थी इसे जानते हैं? हाँ/नहीं
  यदि हाँ, तो किन फायदों के बारे में जानते हैं, यदि नहीं, तो क्यों नहीं जानते हैं?

- आप के विचार से जूनियर हाई स्कूल तक के विद्यार्थी काम के प्रति किस प्रकार की धारणा रखते हैं?

- विद्यार्थियों के घर में लोग काम करते होंगे, जिससे परिवार की आजीविका चलती होगी। आपके विचार से विद्यार्थी इसे कितनी गम्भीरता से समझ पाते होंगे?

- आपके विचार से ऐसे विद्यार्थी अपने भावी जीवन में किस प्रकार के कार्य करने की इच्छा रखते होंगे?

- क्या ऐसे विद्यार्थी, जिनके घर में सभी नौकरी करते हैं, उनसे प्रभावित होकर अधिक मेहनत करते हैं?

- आपके विचार से शारीरिक श्रम पर आधारित कार्यों के जो लाभ होते हैं क्या उन्हें विद्यार्थी समझते हैं? हाँ/नहीं
  यदि हाँ, तो विद्यार्थी ऐसे किन लाभों को समझते हैं। यदि नहीं, तो क्यों नहीं समझते होंगे?

- जो शिक्षा जूनियर हाई स्कूल के बच्चों को दी जा रही है, वह शिक्षा बच्चों को काम के महत्त्व के सम्बन्ध में क्या बताती है?

- आपके विचार से जूनियर हाई स्कूल के विद्यार्थियों को काम के महत्त्व के बारे में बतलाने के लिए क्रियात्मक तरीके (काम कराकर) को महत्त्व देना चाहिये या सैद्धान्तिक (समझाने-बुझाने) तरीकों का?

- बच्चों को जो भी गृह कार्य दिया जाता है कुछ बच्चे उसे उत्साह से पूरा कर लेते हैं और कुछ हमेशा लापरवाही बरतते हैं। आपके विचार से जो विद्यार्थी उत्साह से अपना कार्य करते हैं उनके पीछे कौन से कारण या प्रेरणायें होती हैं?

- इसी प्रकार जो विद्यार्थी अपना कार्य नहीं करते, आपके विचार से उनके काम न करने के क्या कारण हो सकते हैं?

- जो विद्यार्थी अपना काम समय से पूरा नहीं करते, उन्हें किस प्रकार समझाना चाहिए?

- आमतौर पर विद्यार्थी गृह कार्य के प्रति कैसी धारणा रखते हैं?

- जूनियर हाई स्कूल के बच्चे किसी कार्य जैसे गृह कार्य को क्यों पूरा करते हैं? क्या वे कार्य के महत्त्व को समझते हैं या किसी दबाव या डांट के कारण पूरा कर लेते हैं?

- आपके विचार से जूनियर हाई स्कूल के बच्चे यदि काम के महत्त्व को नहीं समझते या गृह कार्य करके नहीं लाते तो इसके लिए कौन ज्यादा जिम्मेदार है, माता-पिता या शिक्षक या वर्तमान शिक्षा प्रणाली?

- आपके विचार में जूनियर हाई स्कूल के बच्चों के कार्यों को किस प्रकार रोचक बनाया जा सकता है?

- आपके विचार से जूनियर हाई स्कूल के बच्चों को कौन सा कार्य दिया जाना चाहिए, जिससे उन्हें कार्य के महत्त्व के बारे में समझने में आसानी हो?

- कुछ ऐसे कार्य बताइये जिनसे जूनियर हाई स्कूल के बच्चों का शारीरिक तथा मानसिक विकास होने में सहायता मिले?

- किसी कार्य को पूरा करने के बाद आनन्द का अनुभव होता है, क्या बच्चे इस आनन्द का अनुभव कर सकते हैं? हाँ/नहीं

APPENDIX-B

Work Values Scale
(For Junior High School Students)

निर्देश

प्रिय बच्चों,

आप लिखते-पढ़ते हैं, खेलते हैं–इसके अलावा भी अन्य प्रकार के अनेक कार्य करते हैं, जैसे घर के कार्य, बाजार के कार्य, इत्यादि। आपके घर के लोग (माता-पिता, भैया, बाबा इत्यादि) भी तरह-तरह के कार्य करते हैं। आपके अड़ोस-पड़ोस के लोग भी कोई न कोई कार्य करते हैं। दरअसल सभी को रोज कुछ न कुछ करना होता है। इसमें से कुछ कामों से कमाई-धमाई होती है जिससे घर-परिवार का काम-काज चलता है, लेकिन कुछ काम 'हाबी' के रूप में भी किये जाते हैं, जैसे जनसेवा का कार्य या श्रमदान का कार्य, इत्यादि। इनसे कोई प्रत्यक्ष कमाई नहीं होती, अपितु इनसे आत्मसन्तोष मिलता है तथा बोरियत से बचाव होता है।

इन कामों के विषय में आप क्या सोचते हैं? यह जानने के लिए हम अब आपसे कुछ प्रश्न पूछेंगे। आप इनके जवाब बिना किसी संकोच के दीजिए। आपके जवाब हम किसी को बतायेंगे नहीं, अतः आपको जो भी जवाब देना हो, खुलकर दीजिए।

धन्यवाद।

S. No.	*Item*	*Response Alternatives*
1.	घर में मम्मी-पापा या घर का कोई बड़ा जब भी आपसे कुछ करने को कहता है तो आप को कैसा लगता है?	बहुत गुस्सा आता है/कुछ नहीं लगता/अच्छा लगता है।
2.	होम वर्क को कितने विद्यार्थी बोझ समझते हैं?	अधिकतर विद्यार्थी/थोड़े बहुत/ कोई नहीं।
3.	स्कूल में दिये गये होम वर्क से क्या होता है?	विद्यार्थी के खाली समय का सदुपयोग/कुछ नहीं। विद्यार्थी के ऊपर बोझ लद जाता है।
4.	घर के जरूरी कार्यों को पूरा करना किसकी जिम्मेदारी है?	परिवार के छोटे-बड़े सभी की/केवल बड़े लोगों की/पता नहीं
5.	मित्रों या पड़ोसी के यहाँ शादी-ब्याह या ऐसे ही किसी अन्य अवसरों पर आप उनके सहयोग में कार्य करने के लिए कितना तत्पर रहते हैं?	बहुत अधिक/थोड़ा बहुत/ बिल्कुल नहीं।
6.	आप कितना विश्वास करते हैं कि जो जितना कार्य करेगा वह उतना ही सफल होगा?	बहुत अधिक/थोड़ा बहुत/ बिल्कुल नहीं।
7.	घर-परिवार में आपको जो भी कार्य सौंपा जाता है, उसे आप कितने मन से पूरा करने का प्रयास करते हैं?	बहुत अधिक/थोड़ा बहुत/ बिल्कुल नहीं।
8.	काम करते समय आप कितनी जल्दी ऊब जाते हैं?	बहुत जल्दी/थोड़ी देर बाद/ काम से नहीं ऊबता।

क्रमशः

S. No.	*Item*	*Response Alternatives*
9.	कोई जिम्मेदारी भरा काम करते समय आपको कितना आनन्द मिलता है?	बहुत अधिक/थोड़ा बहुत/ बिल्कुल नहीं।
10.	जिसे जो कार्य सौंपा जाए उसे वह अपना कर्तव्य समझ कर पूरा करे। इससे आप कितना सहमत हैं।	बहुत अधिक/थोड़ा बहुत/ बिल्कुल नहीं।
11.	अपना भविष्य अच्छा बनाने के लिए व्यक्ति को कार्य करना ही पड़ता है?	सही/पता नहीं/गलत।
12.	जो काम आपको करने को दिया गया होता है, उसे पूरा करने पर आपको कैसा लगता है?	लगता है कि बोझ उतर गया/ कुछ नहीं लगता।
13.	मान लीजिए कि आपके घर-परिवार में कोई भी काम न करता तो क्या होता?	लोग बैठकर गप्प लड़ाकर मजा लेते/पता नहीं/घर में सुख-सुविधा खत्म हो जाती।
14.	यदि किसी को अपना भविष्य अच्छा बनाना है तो उसे काम करना ही होगा?	सही/पता नहीं/गलत।

निम्नलिखित कार्यों के प्रति अपनी पसन्दगी बताइये:–

15.	घर के काम जैसे-सामान लाना, घर की सफाई	पसन्द/न पसन्द न नापसन्द/ नापसन्द।
16.	पढ़ाई-लिखाई का काम	पसन्द/न पसन्द न नापसन्द/ नापसन्द।
17.	ऐसे काम करना जिससे ज्ञान बढ़े	पसन्द/न पसन्द न नापसन्द/ नापसन्द।

क्रमशः

S. No.	*Item*	*Response Alternatives*
18.	आपको होम वर्क या अन्य जो भी कार्य दिया जाता है, आप उसे कितना पूरा करते हैं?	अक्सर पूरा करता हूँ/थोड़ा बहुत/पूरा हो न हो परवाह नहीं करता।
अपना होमवर्क या अन्य कार्य आप क्यों पूरा करते हैं?		
19.	इससे ज्ञान पढ़ता है तथा विकास होता है	सही/अनिश्चित/गलत।
20.	आप अपना होम वर्क खुद करते हैं या घर के बड़े या माता-पिता से करवाते हैं?	घर के लोगों से करवाता हूँ/ पूरा होम वर्क स्वयं करता हूँ।
21.	क्या आपको ऐसा लगता है कि जो होम वर्क आपको दिया जा रहा है उसके कारण आपको खेलने का समय नहीं मिल पा रहा है?	हाँ/अनिश्चित/नहीं।
22.	आपको घर का काम न करना पड़े इसके लिए आप अक्सर स्कूल से मिले होम वर्क करने का बहाना बनाते हैं?	हाँ/अनिश्चित/नहीं।
23.	घर के बुजुर्ग जैसे दादा-दादी की सेवा करना आपको कैसा लगता है?	बहुत अच्छा लगता है/कम अच्छा लगता है/बिल्कुल भी अच्छा नहीं लगता।
24.	यदि आप किसी को अधिक मेहनत करके सफल होते हुए देखते हैं तो क्या आप सोचते हैं कि आपको भी उसी की तरह मेहनत करनी चाहिए?	हाँ/अनिश्चित/नहीं।

क्रमशः

S. No.	*Item*	*Response Alternatives*
25.	यदि कोई बहुत अमीर व्यक्ति है तो भी क्या उसे कार्य करना चाहिए?	हाँ/अनिश्चित/नहीं।
26.	किसी काम में असफल होने पर आपको कितना बुरा लगता है?	बहुत बुरा लगता है/थोड़ा बुरा लगता है/ बिल्कुल बुरा नहीं लगता।

Bibliography

Abu-Saad, I. and Isralowitz, R.E. (1997). Gender as a Determinant of Work Values among University Students in Israel. *Journal of Social Psychology*, 137, 749-763.

Achenbach, T. and Howell, C. (1993). 'Are American Children's Problems getting worse? A 13-year comparison. *Journal of the American Academy of Child and Adolescent Psychiatry*, 32(6), 1145-1154.

Allport, W; Vernon, P.E.; and Lindzey, G. (1960). *Allport-Vernon-Lindzey Study of Values* (3rd ed.). Boston: H.M.

Baumeister, R.F. and Exline, J.J. (1999). Virtue, Personality and Social Relations: Self Control as the Moral Muscle, *Journal of Personality*, 67(6),1165-1194.

Bedley, G. (2003). *Cultivating Values in Middle School Kids*. California: National Character Education Centre Publication.

Chilana, M.R. and Dewan (2002). *The Human Values: A Task for All*. New Delhi: Concept Publishing Company.

Dawis, R.V. (2001). 1999 Leona Tyler Award: Rene V. Dawis. *Counselling Psychologists*, 29.458-465.

Deb, T. (2008). *Human Resource Development: Theories and Practice*. New Delhi: Ane Books Pvt. Ltd.

Dewey, J. (1916). *Democracy and Education*. New York: McMillan.

Dhar, C. (1985). Work Values of Adolescent Boys. *Guidance Review*, 3(1), 12-21.

Drenth, P.J.D.; Thierry, H.; Willems, P.J. and de Wolff, C.J. (1984). *Handbook of Work and Organizational Behaviour* (Vol. 1). John Willey & Sons Ltd.

Duffy, R.D. and Sedlacek, W.E. (2007). The Work Values of First-Year College Students: Exploring Group Differences. *Career Development Quarterly* (June).

Freud, S. (1930). *Civilization and its Discontents.* London: Hogarth Press.

Friedlander, F. (2006). Comparative Work Value Systems. *Personnel Psychology*, 18(1), 1-20.

Furth, H.G. (1996). Human Mind in Human Society. *Human Development*, 39, 264-268.

Gaebarino, J. (1998). Raising Children in a Socially Toxic Environment. *Family Matters*, No. 50, 53-55.

Ganesh, S.R. (1982). *Quality of Life in Indian Organization: An Irrelevant View.* I.I.M., Ahmedabad, W.P. No. 407.

Goldstein, B. and Oldham, J. (1979). *Children and Work: A Study of Socialization.* New Brunswick, New Jersey: Transaction Books.

Gupta, N.L. (2002). *Human Values in Education.* New Delhi: Mittal Pub.

Herzberg, F. (1966). *The Motivation to Work.* New York: Harper.

Jahoda, M. (1981). Work, Employment and Unemployment. *American Psychologists,* 36, 184-191.

Johnson, M.K. (2001). Job Values in the Young Adult Transition: Stability and Change with Age. *Social Psychology Quarterly*, 64, 297-317.

Johnson, M.K. (2002). Social Origins, Adolescent Experiences, and Work Value Trajectories during the Transition to Adulthood. *Social Forces*, 80(4), 1307-1340.

Johnson, M.K. (2005). Family Roles and Work Values: Processes of Selection and Change. *Journal of Marriage and Family*, 67, 352-369.

Kaestle, C.F. (1978). Social Change, Discipline and the Common School in Early Nineteenth-Century America. *The Journal of Interdisciplinary History*, 9(1), pp. 1-17.

Kahn, R.L. (1981). *Work and Health.* New York: John Willey.

Kaiser, C.R.; Major, B. and McCoy (2004). Expectations about the Future and the Emotional Consequences of Percsiving Prejudice. *Personality and Social Psychology Bulletin,* 30, 173-184.

Karr, N.N. (1996). *Value Education: A Philosophical Study*. Ambala: The Associated Publishers.

Kaur, R. and Singh, K. (2000). Psychological Correlates of Organizational Commitment. *Personality Study and Group Behaviour*, 20, 103-115.

Kohlberg, L. (1964). Development of Moral Character and Moral Ideology, pp. 383-431. In L.W. Hoffman and M.L. Hoffman (eds.). *Review of Child Development Research* (Vol. 1). New York: Russell Sage Foundation.

Leong, F.T.L. and Tata, S.P. (1990). Sex and Acculturation Differences in Occupational Values among Chinese-American Children. *Journal of Counselling Psychology*, 37(2), 208-212.

Lindsay, P. and Knox (1984). Continuity and Change in Work Values among Adults: A Longitudinal study. *The American Journal of Sociology*, 89(4), pp. 918-931.

Liu, Y. and Lei, Y. (2012). The Connotation of Work Values: A Preliminary Review. *Asian Social Science*, 8(1), 47-53.

Loughlin, C.A. and Barling, J. (1998). Teenagers' Part-Time Employment and their Work-related Attitudes and Aspirations. *Journal of Organizational Behaviour,* 19(2), pp. 197-207.

Luzzo, D.A. (2000). *Career Counselling of College Students: An Empirical Guide to Strategies that Work.* Washington, DC.: American Psychological Association.

Marini, M.M.; Pi-Ling, F.; Erica, F.; and Ann, M.B. (1996). Gender and Job Values. *Sociology of Education*, 74, 884-901.

McClelland, D.C. (1961). *The Achieving Society*. New York: Free Press.

McLoyd, V.C. (1989). Socialization and Development in a Changing Economy: The Effects of Paternal Job and Income Loss on Children. *American Psychologist,* 44(2),293-302.

McLoyd, V.C. (1990). The Impact of Economic Hardship on Black Families and Children: Psychological Distress, Parenting and Socio-Emotional Development. *Child Development,* 61(2), 311-346.

Mehta, P. (1994). *Social Achievement Motivation: Needs, Values and Work Organization.* New Delhi: Concept Publishing Company.

Miceli, M. and Castlefrenchi, C. (2002). The Mind and the Future: The Power of Expectations. *Theory Psychology*, 12, 335-366.

Mirowsky, J. (2011). Wage Slavery or Creative Work. *Society and Mental Health,* 1(2), 73-88.

Mishra C. (1994). Developing Work Culture. *Indian Journal of Industrial Relations*. 29(3). 335-338.

Mitra, A. (2007). *Kaash Ham Bachhon Ko Sawal Puchhana Sikhate.* Lucknow; Hindustan, September, 18.

Monica, K.J. (2005). Family Roles and Work Values: Processes of Selection and Change. *Journal of Marriage and Family*, 67(2), 352-369.

Mortimer, J.T. (1996). Social Psychological Aspects of Achievement. In A.C. Kerkoff (ed.) *In Generating Social Stratification: Toward A New Research Agenda,* pp. 17-36. West View Press.

Mortimer, J.T. and Lorence, J. (1979). Occupational Experience and the Self Concept: A Longitudinal Study. *Social Psychology Quarterly*, 42, 307-323.

Mortimer, J.T.; Pimentel, E.E.; Ryu, S.; Nash, K. and Lee C. (1996). Part-Time Work and Occupational Value Formation in Adolescence. *Social Forces*, 74(4), pp. 1405-1418.

Nag, M; White, B.N.F.; and Peet, R.C. (1978). An Anthropological Approach to the Study of the Economic Value of Children in Java and Nepal. *Current Anthropology*, 19(2), 293-306.

Neumann, L. and Neumann, Y. (1983). A Discriminant Analysis of Students' Work Values: Differences between Engineering and Liberal Arts. *Journal of Experimental Education*, 52, 40-45.

Nnaike, U. (2008). Instill values in students. (*Retrived from http://www.thisdayonline.com, Nigeria News*, 13-11-2008.)

Nye, F.L. and Hoffman, L. (1974). *Working Mothers*. San Francisco: Jossey Boss.

Palsane, M.N. and Lam, D.J. (1996). Stress and Coping from Traditional Indian and Chinese Perspectives. *Psychology and Developing Societies*, 8(1), 29-53.

Pandey, N. and Naidu, R.K. (1992). *Anasakti* and Health: A Study of Nonattachment. *Psychology and Developing Societies*, 4, 89-104.

Pandian, C. (2005). Teach Human Values to University Students. *The Hindu*. (*Retrived from http://www.thehindu.com, 19-06-2005.*)

Paranjpe, A.C. (2002). Indigenous Psychology in the Post-Colonial Context: An Historical Perspective. *Psychology and Developing Societies*, 14(1), 27-44.

Parker, S.R. and Smith, M.A (1976). Work and Leisure. In R. Dubin (ed.), *Handbook of Work, Organization and Society*. Chicago: Rand McNally.

Patil, V.T. (2008). *Value Education and Human Rights Education*. Delhi: GNOSIS.

Perrone, K.; Selacek, W.E. and Alexander, C.M. (2001). Gender and Ethnic Differences in Career Goal Attainment. *The Career Development Quarterly*, 50, 168-178.

Ravlin, E.C. and Meglino, B.M. (1987). Effect of Values on Perception and Decision Making: A Study of Alternative Work Values Measures. *Journal of Applied Psychology*, 12(4), 666-673.

Rawat, H.K. (2007). *Sociology: Basic Concepts*. Jaipur: Rawat Publication.

Rodgers, D.T. (1980). Socializing Middle-Class Children: Institutions, Fables, and Work Values in Nineteenth-Century America. *Journal of Social History*, 13(3), 353-367.

Rogoff, B. (1990). *Apprenticeship in Thinking: Cognitive Development in Social Context*. New York: Oxford University Press.

Rogoff, B.; Mistry, J.; Goncu, A. and Mosier, C. (1993). Guided participation in cultural activity by toddlers and caregivers. *Monograph of the Society for Research in Child Development*, 58(8), Serial No. 236).

Rohmetra, N. (2000). Cultural Diversity and Ethical Behaviour at Work Place—an Analysis. *Indian Journal of Industrial Relations*, 35(3), 301-305.

Rokeach, M. (1973). *The Nature of Human Values*. New York: Free Press.

Roy, P. (1961). Maternal Employment and Adolescent Roles: Rural-Urban Differences. *Marriage and Family Living*, 23 (November), 340-349.

Sagy, S. (1997). Work values: Comparing Russian Immigrants and Israeli Students. *Journal of Career Development*, 23(*3*), 231-235.

Salemela-Aro, K.; Tolvanen, A.; and Nurmi, J. (2009). Achievement Strategies during University Studies Predict Early Career Burnout and Engagement. *Journal of Vocational Behaviour*, 75 (*2*), 162-172

Sandhu, V. and Tewari, M. (2007). Are You the Best Parent You Can Be? Lucknow: *Sunday Hindustan Times*, January, 14.

Schein, E.H. (1985). *Organizational Culture and Leadership*. San Francisco: Jossey-Bass.

Scott, C.D.; Jaffe, D.T.; and Tobe, G.R. (2004). *Organizational Vision, Values and Mission*. New Delhi: Viva Books Pvt. Ltd.

Segal, R. (1966). *The Crisis of India*. New York: Library Publication.

Shukla, R.P. (2004). *Value Education and Human Rights Education*. New Delhi: Sarup & Sons.

Shukla, S. (2004). Human Values and Environment. In K.M. Mahapatra (ed.) *Technology Environment and Human Values*. New Delhi: Concept Publishing Company, pp. 139-141.

Silcock, P.J. and Wyness, M. (2000). Dedicated to their Work: Primary School Children Talk about their Curriculum. *Curriculm*, 21(*2*).

Silvino, P.J. (1996). A study of the Values of Elementary School Children. *Education*, 96 (2), 170-176.

Singh, S. (1999). Organizational Behaviour and Work Values. In U.N.Dash and U. Jain (eds.). *Perspectives on Psychology and Social Development*. New Delhi: Concept Publishing Company.

Sinha, J.B.P. (1977a). The Poverty Syndrome, Power Motive, and Democratization of Work Place. *Integrated Management*, 12, 5-8.

Sinha, J.B.P. (1977b). The Quality of Working Life in the Indian Setting. *Journal of Social and Economic Studies*,.5, 235-248.

Sinha, J.B.P. (1990). The Salient Indian Values and Their Socio-Ecological Roots. *Indian Journal of Social Sciences*, 3, 477-488.

Sinha, J.B.P. (1990). *Work Culture in the Indian Context*. Sage: New Delhi.

Sinha, J.B.P. (1994). Form Soft to Synergetic Work Culture. *Indian Journal of Industrial Relations*, 29(*3*), 291-302.

Sinha, J.B.P. (2008). Living and Doing Psychology. Paper presented in Symposium on *Indian Psychology: Theory, Methods and Trends* during the NAOP Conference at the IIT, Guwahati on December 14-17.

Sir Shree (2011). "Rukata nahin karma ka pahiya". *Dainik Jagaran*, August, 21.

Smith, C.P. (1969). The Origin an Expression of Achievement-related Motives in Children. In C.P. Smith (ed.) *Achievement related motives in children*. New York: Russell Sage Foundation, pp. 102-150.

St. Claire, L.; Hayward, R.; and Rogers, P. (2010). Interactive Effects of Caffeine Consumption and Stressful Circumstances on Components of Stress: Caffeine Makes Men Less, But Women More Effective as Partners Under Stress. *Journal of Applied Social Psychology*, 40 (12), 3106-3129.

Staff, J. and Mortimer, J.T. (2007), Educational and Work Strategies from Adolescence to Early Adulthood: Consequences for Educational Attainment. *Social Forces*, 85(3), pp. 1169-1194.

Steers, R.M. and Porter, L.W. (1979). *Motivation and Work Behaviour*. New York: McGraw Hill.

Strauss, M.A. (1962). Work Roles and Financial Responsibility in the Socialization of Farm, Fringe, and Town Boys. *Rural Sociology*, 27 (September), 257-274.

Strong, R.; Silver, H.F.; and Robinson, A. (1995). What Do Students Want (and What Really Motivate Them)? *Educational Leadership*, September.

Suar, D. (1992). Work Values of Managers and Workers. *Indian Journal of Applied Psychology*. 29.(1).

Tan, K.C. and Khoo, H.H. (2002). Indian Society, Total Quality and the Rajiv Gandhi National Quality Award. *Jovrnal of Management Development,* 21(6),417-426.

Tiwari, A.K. (2000). Anasakti and Mental Health. *Psychological Studies*, 45(3), 156-160.

Tiwari, A.K. (2003). *Indigenous Conceptualization of Two Types of Beliefs: In search of Psychological Determinants of a System-Failure.* Unpublished Project Report, UGC, New Delhi.

Tiwari, A.K. (2007). Crystallized India for Development. In M.B. Sharan and D. Suar (eds.) *Psychology Matters: Development, Health and Organization*. New Delhi: Allied Publishers.

Underwood, B.J. (1955). *Experimental Psychology: An Introduction*. Indian Edition.

Vasantha, A. (1971). *A Study of Work Values of Higher Secondary Students of Delhi in relation to their Intelligence, Achievement and Socio-Economic Status.* Doctoral Dissertation in Education, University of Delhi.

Venkatraman, G. (2007). "Totaratant se vicharshilata ki or". Lucknow; *Hindustan*, September, 18.

Warr, P. (1984). Work and Employment. In P.J.D. Drenth, H. Thierry, P.J. Willems, and C.J. de Wolff (eds.). *Handbook of Work and Organizational Behaviour* (Vol. 1). John Willey & Sons Ltd.

Weisgram, E.S. (2006). *Gender, Values, and the Formation of Occupational Goals.* Dissertation submitted for Doctor of Philosophy, The University of Texas at Austin.

Weisgram, E.S.; Bigler, R.S. and Liben, L.S. (2010). Gender, Values, and Occupational Interests among Children, Adolescents, and Adults. *Child Development*, Volume 81, Number *3*, Pages 778-796.

White, L.K. and Brinkerhoff, D.B. (1981). Children's Work in the Family: Its Significance and Meaning. *Journal of Marriage and the Family*, 43(4), 789-798.

Wollack, S.; Goodale, J.G.; Wijting, J.P. and Smith, P.C. (1971). Development of the Survey of Work Values. *Journal of Applied Psychology*, 55(4), 331-338.

Yu, Y.H. and Li, Z. (2003). Research on the Feature of Work Values and Educational Counter Measure for Contemporary College Students (in Chinese). *Education Exploration*, 12, 42-44.

Index